One Man's Island

LOOKING TOWARD FERNWOOD

One Man's Island

by David Conover

GENERAL PUBLISHING COMPANY LIMITED
TORONTO

Also by DAVID CONOVER

Once Upon an Island

Photographs by the author

Copyright © David Conover, 1971

General Publishing Company Limited
30 Lesmill Road, Don Mills, Ontario

ISBN—0-7736-0016-7

Printed in the United States of America

To
WILL DAWSON,
who
believed

Contents

Acknowledgment

I wish to thank Anne Conover Ambrose
for her criticism and her many valuable suggestions.

Spring

This may be a calendar of the ebbs and flows of the soul; and on these sheets as a beach, the waves may cast up pearls and seaweed.

H. D. Thoreau

MAPLE SEED DUSTERS

IT IS TRUE, as Alfred De Vigny says, "A fine life is a thought conceived in youth and realized in maturity." As a youth I had one strong desire: to lead an outdoor life. Why, I am not sure. Freedom, perhaps. City streets always impressed me as flat walls, and I found myself invariably drawn to the open desert and the wild wasteland of Baja California, the

> Solitary places where we taste
> The pleasure of believing all we see
> Is boundless, as we wish our souls to be. *

Yet the outdoors—no matter how beautiful—never held my interest long without the sight of the sea. The rolling waves breaking upon some sparse, deserted beach appeased an obscure hunger within me. Weekends became outdoor pilgrimages to the sand dunes of Ensenada and the untrodden beaches of Cape Colnett. We camped and played, ate and sang, made

* Van Wyck Brooks

3

love, slept, and dreamed—waking to the sea invading our sleeping bags or the coyotes baying at the moon.

Surf and stars, happiness and freedom, I discovered, were one and the same. With nature, I felt a certain completeness—the joyful awareness of being alive.

For twenty-four citybound years, I had confused happiness with pleasure. But happiness is not complete without joy. And joy was what my life was sadly lacking. Each working morning I wanted to stay in bed. Only the quest for pleasure, for "fun," seemed to kill the burden of living. I was already a successful photographer, yet I had the feeling I was missing something; that I could do more, *be* more— The words of a wonderful teacher, Allan Dartford, persisted in my head: "Life is a petty thing unless there is an urge to expand its boundaries."

My heart held an island.

I would be called upon to build our own house, find water, grow our own food, secure fuel and lumber from the forest, and—if need be—make our own clothing; to know and become familiar with the real essentials of life of which, as a city dweller, I was totally ignorant. For income, we would build a resort. A few simple cottages. That was my dream —if Jeanne was willing.

"Shall we risk it?" I asked breathlessly.

She smiled. "Why not—we're young, healthy, and strong."

And so we did.

TO LIVE ON AN ISLAND is to awaken to a world so peaceful that spotting an oyster catcher is an exciting event.

A brisk, sea-foamed March day. I battle a bumpy channel to Fernwood and go into Ganges after much-needed supplies. How good it is to get a hello from passing cars, to see familiar faces in Mouat's Store—to know the life behind every smile.

In the city, one shops alone.

At the hardware counter and in the feed shed, I get caught up with the human family, and today I found it difficult to break away for home.

THOSE WHO FACE the weather rarely have to face the doctor. There is truth to this, as any countryman will testify. Vic Bettiss has not been off his feet since the youthful day he set foot on Salt Spring. To him there's no such thing as bad weather. When I first came here I was alarmed by the continual leak in the sky.

"What do you do when it rains?" I asked him.

"Pretend it ain't," he shot back.

The wind and rain make the pulse beat vigorously. They warm the blood and quicken the mind. The wood Vic collects in the storm heats him twice. He staggers into the room with a ten-foot log, then spends the evening poking it into the fire. "Cuttin' it up," he declares, "is jist a waste of time, son."

He harvests his strength as he does his crops. At milking time—always at night, for he claims the days "weren't made fer sittin'"—his cows come to the door. Their plaintive calls arouse him from his catnap and drive him to the barn, where by lantern light he fills the pails with ivory liquid. Swish, swish! His hands are tireless pistons and his eyes are as grave and distant as those of a broody hen.

"Why do you like milking, Vic?" I wanted to know. "You don't drink the stuff, and you said it doesn't pay."

He glanced up.

"Gives me time to think, son."

His cows hear his weary truck a mile away and are at the gate, waiting patiently to feel his gentle hand stroke their heads. He is slave to his cows, chickens, cats, pigs, and sheep —but never to machines. When the Rototiller stops, he explodes, cursing it so vociferously it starts up from sheer fright. Then, minutes later, with boyish pride he'll spout its praises— as if it had never stopped. Though he is childless, his days are filled with children. Each morning when he swings open the school-bus doors, his smile is as wide as his love. To him, no job pays so well for so small a check.

His book knowledge, he admits, is as "scarce as mice in the barn," yet every Salter knows whom to call to treat a sick ewe, fix a pump, put out a chimney fire, unplug a septic tank, build a barn, or set a Labrador's broken leg. His love for people is a thirst even greater than for good rye. Their troubles are never a problem to him—only to Myrt. "If it weren't for the cows," she confided once, "he'd firget to come home." He sticks to every job long after the wage has been earned. He is never in a hurry, never finds time to fret. When he installed Ernie Burr's toilet, it was six weeks before he got around to hooking up the water. For him—God bless him— the moment is world enough.

EVERYONE, it seems, knows how to earn a living. But does anyone know how to spend it?

MARCH SNEAKED by like a thief, stealing from us hours of leisure and beauty. Everywhere westerly winds have made us run for the hammer or axe, rake or peavey. Cottage roofs are minus shingles, the orchard is strewn with branches, and trails are jammed with windfalls and debris. Now as I look from the window, the gangway is off its runners, and logs litter every foot of the beaches. Oh, March—you brute, I'm glad you come only once a year!

Last night I read Keats's letters till midnight—wishing to mark every line. As Napoleon said of Goethe: *"Voilà un homme!"* I am dazzled by the richness of his nature, by the grasp of his intellect and feeling, by the extraordinary powers of friendship and awareness of one who died still a youth. With men like this, no wonder so small a country as England could conquer a quarter of the globe, then relinquish it with honor.

SNOW IS STILL on Vancouver Island, but the air is warm and fragrant with the scent of low tide. In shirt sleeves, I finished pruning the apple trees and raked the yard. I love working with my hands. Like Vic's milking, it "gives me time to think." Sometimes this is neither good for apple production—nor wise. While shingling the other day, I forgot where the roof left off. Jeanne helped me to my feet, and seeing that I was unharmed, scolded, "You nut, save your writing for the desk."

Why this hunger to write—I always ask myself—if not the longing to discover what I believe? The pen divines my thoughts.

All day I have been thinking of the great advances of mankind since the turn of the century, and how paradoxical it is that each step of technology and enlightenment has, in its turn, rendered the individual more helpless, dependent, and fearful.

We have become leaners—leaning on our families, our tradesmen, our towns, our state, our country, our President. Where is the man who stands on his own two feet—ethically, morally, and humanly? The man who says "To hell with you," and goes about his business? In the rush for progress I wonder if we have not lost the sense of what it is to be a man. Science deluges us with gifts, which by drip and trickle erode the human spirit. Where once we stood, strong and sufficient, we bend like twigs before every wind of convenience. We forget that the most important thing to come off the production line is not the Ford. Progress is big business. But our real business is living. Show me the man who has made the most profitable knowledge of himself—that is the highest rung of progress.

APRIL is a spoiled child—an elusive blessing or a curse. One day it's raw and windy; the next, warm and shining. Each morning we are faced with a weighty decision. Should we put on our long johns or leave them off?

The first geese journeyed over the island yesterday. They brought the clear, sparkling air. There's a nip in the shade, where winter still reigns, but the yard is sun-filled and the grass ankle deep, diamonded with dew. No four walls could hold me inside. Jeanne was starting the mower. "Let's go fishing," I pleaded. "To hell with the grass!"

A spring tonic! No need for it here. We open the window and take a deep breath.

I AM INTOLERABLY WEALTHY—so rich I cannot begin to spend my blessings. But I forget to enjoy. To relax by the cove in a Cape Cod chair and forget there is so much to do. It's like running after a train in a dream—we can't quite reach it. We have one foot in the future, the other in the past, while the body goes through the motions of living. We're too busy either readying for summer or preparing for winter. The true enjoyment of each eludes us. Happiness, it seems, is shy. Not until after it's gone do we know that we have experienced it. Perhaps we live too much in the future. How often I hear it said, "We'll take that trip later—perhaps next year—when my husband retires." There is only one moment we are sure of. Now!

"It might be good for us," writes John Fowles in *The*

THE THREE OF US

Aristos, "if we learned the exact year that our particular world will end. We would then begin to understand the *now.*"

What an incredible memory! I can't remember a thing unless I jot it down. Fortunately, my journals are extensions of my mind. They raise me above myself. Without them, my thoughts would perish, and I'd be reduced to a very humdrum existence.

More resort inquiries. Mr. Hudson asks if he can bring his poodle. With Kiki? For his dog's sake, NO!

THIS MORNING Jeanne found a sand dollar on the beach. She had never seen one. Inside, like brittle pieces of porcelain, were five tiny doves. She held them up excitedly. "They must be something special, like pearls. What are they?"

"Teeth," I said, hating to disappoint her.

Jeanne frowned.

"How unromantic. Wish you hadn't told me." Her soft green eyes studied them again. "They don't seem nearly as beautiful."

A little ignorance is a wholesome thing. "When you give a child the name of the bird," said Joyce Cary, "it loses the bird. It never sees the bird again but only a sparrow, a thrush, a swan." Nature's fascination lies in our wonder. I have no desire to lift her veil—only to take each phenomenon as it comes, without straining for fact or reason, careless whether it is a sunrise, a flower, or a man.

I love April—its greenness, eagerness, and growth— except when I face the blasted lawn!

How often a woman sees things more clearly than a man. Jeanne quickly gets down to essentials. The other day while I was replacing several blown-off shingles—the asphalt kind that flap in the wind—Jeanne said, "Put a little tar on them, Dave. Then they won't curl or blow off so easily." How handy it is to have a woman around!

Yet a woman never wants a man underfoot. Her day is seriously impeded with a husband in the house. She must have privacy to do those inconsequential duties that a male would only sneer or chuckle at. My solution—a den in the lumber shed. This morning Jeanne hastened my departure with the comment, "That's enough toast. You know it makes you gain weight." A signal to get moving. So before impatience descends, I am out the door. Here in the den I write inconsequentials while Jeanne is doing them.

NOTHING SPOILS intelligence like a paltry heart. Logic is no cure-all for mankind's ills. Or a man's. We know too much, understand too little. Speak logic to an upset woman, you breed a hurricane. She doesn't want reason—all she wants is heart!

What cannot be reasoned is work for the heart. I met this situation headlong last year when our taxes were doubled. Our livelihood, our home—even the island—was threatened. The resort business, plainly marginal, could not stand such a blow. For weeks we were depressed. We consulted friends, businessmen, lawyers. . . . There were no grounds to win an appeal. Reason, we were told, could not budge British Law. Fortunately, the day the appeal court met in Ganges, the heart had ways the mind does not perceive. It saw a way, when I presented our case, to move a judge to reduce the unjust burden.

WHAT DAYS OF APRIL beauty are these! So sharp, clear, and still that you cannot believe them real. This afternoon, while Davey napped, we hied ourselves briskly and bareheaded to Chivers' Point. It was a billy-goat scramble, up sharp cliffs of sandstone and sliding—sometimes falling—down slopes slippery with madrona leaves, yet not once did we feel fatigued. We came home with a sense of exultation, built a fire, and drank hot coffee. After dinner I read several chapters of *Wind in the Willows* to Davey, and when he had gone to bed, we listened to Sibelius and the crackling of logs and knew —after we loved in the firelight—that this had been a wondrous day.

These mornings when I awake, I thank God for the gift of life. I wonder: Am I proving worthy of it?

The dictionary defines *living* as: "Alive; having life; not dead; full of vigor; gushing forth; flowing as a living stream." How many of us fit this description?

THERE IS SOMETHING very beautiful about Rachel Carson's tragic story. Why did she dedicate the last four years of her life to writing *Silent Spring,* a book definitely not of her choosing, when she could have been traveling or living as she pleased? Certainly not for wealth. Not for fame or prestige. She had all these. "The worth of goodness is most striking," wrote Matthew Arnold in his admirable essay on Marcus Aurelius, "which is borne by those to whom all the means of pleasure and self-indulgence lay open." Every fine author, like Rachel Carson, is in some degree a spiritual physician —a giver of new life, often at the cost of his own.

The difficulty of talent is to make one's life measure up to its demands. "The best you can write," said Thoreau, "will be the best you are." For the same difficulties that impede one in life impede one in creation. If I am to become a better writer, I must first become a better man.

Words I love: *promise, skill, ardor, intensity, growth.*

The joy of creation stems not from accomplishment but

from the satisfaction gained from the state of being that makes accomplishment inevitable.

"Why does Papa go to the shed?" Davey asked his mother.

"To work, dear. He's writing a book."

"Why?"

"Because he wants to."

"Why does he want to, Mom? We've got so many."

When I go into the woods, I carry no bird book, binoculars, or gun, though often a camera—as I try to leave the mind's paraphernalia at the house, too. This makes me light with weight as with opinion, so that I may soak up all the wilderness my pores will hold.

The beauty of the forest humanizes me. Among the salal, the shy lady-slipper is a flower of thought and feeling that, Hawthorne once said, seems to have its roots deep in the hearts of those who gaze upon it.

YESTERDAY WE MET the freight truck at Fernwood and brought over the "fridge."

"She's beautiful," Jeanne exclaimed, surveying the four-hundred-pound box that barely squeezed through the door. "Not a scratch anywhere." After manhandling it in and out of the launch, dragging it up to the house on a cart, this was miraculous.

"Hold your breath, honey. I'll fire her up."

We were excited. Nine years without firm Jell-o or ice cream was long enough.

The instructions were simple. The Servel booklet said, "Turn the valve on, press the pilot button, and light the burner." The burner clicked on. Every few minutes we opened the door to feel if the box was getting cold. After an hour, not a sign. Several hours slipped by; still no frost on the coils.

Grumbling and disappointed, we went to bed, wondering what was wrong.

This morning I moved the fridge from the wall, took off the rear cover, and inspected the maze of pipes and coils. Everything appeared all right.

I shook my head. "We'll have to call the service department. Maybe they'll send someone out."

Over the radiophone, we explained our plight. "You must understand," the serviceman said, "that if it was damaged en route, we are not responsible. But I'll try to catch the ten o'clock ferry."

When he arrived, he lit the burner. We waited. Not a breath of cold air.

"I know the trouble," he said cheerfully. "Give me a hand, we'll roll her on the floor."

"On the floor?" We were stunned.

"Yes. It'll force the refrigerant back to where it belongs."

On blankets and rugs, we rolled it over several times, then hooked it up again. Lo and behold, it started to frost.

He turned to us. "You must have laid it on its side bringing it over. I'll have to charge you for this call." He pulled out a note pad and figured. "Counting mileage and ferries, that'll be thirty-seven fifty."

Lesson: When you see something marked: KEEP THIS END UP—for goodness sake, *keep it up!*

Listened to Chopin's Nocturnes this evening. I am like a bear in a hive of honey—every note is delicious.

WHILE IN VANCOUVER not long ago I visited a friend who runs a pet shop. He is a handsome man, blond and robust with a Nordic complexion, sensitive lips, and intense blue eyes. His boyish vigor and great love of life attracted me to him. As I sat in his living room, I noticed they were absent, and boredom glazed his eyes. Had he lost interest in his shop? I wondered.

I asked him.

"No—not really. I can't complain, Dave. It makes us a good living. But cleaning up after those animals gets awful tiresome. And we're so tied down we can't go anywhere."

A successful business does not mean a successful life. Too often, as in Collin's case, it ends up blocking life. Without a creative outlet, the human machine either boils over or breaks down. I was fearful for Collin. At dinner I put a bug in his craw.

"With your amusing experiences, Collin, why don't you write a book?"

"Are you nuts?" He laughed. "I didn't even pass Freshman English."

I pointed out that I hadn't fared better, that even Edison failed as a student, that most writers came from other professions. "Besides," I added, "your letters prove you can write. Why, that episode about retrieving the monkey from atop the church steeple is hilarious."

I drove my point home with such conviction that his wife broke in, "Darling, at least you can try."

Collin is a man who basically loves a challenge. His eyes brightened. "All right, I will."

He's got his wife in the store now, and he's been pounding the typewriter ever since. When love, labor, and skill unite—look out!

IN MAKING LOVE, or making a dessert, I am the constant novice. When I am not learning I know I am not living. The tragedy of life is our inability to grow, to change, to stretch. Each day beckons me to enlarge myself. I wire or shingle a cottage in the morning; make camera studies, repair a wharf or a generator, and catch a salmon in the afternoon; write a chapter, study the Greeks, or create a poem at night. My curiosity keeps me in a perpetual state of adolescence. Every tool I see I wish to use; every skill I wish to practice. Living is so exciting, I find it difficult to apply myself to any other occupation.

We have been going over the pile of drift lumber, with an eye toward building another float. Jeanne figures the moorage will bring in at least ninety dollars a season.

"We've got the lumber," she insisted. "And the logs are free."

"Good," I remarked. "When do you start?" I like to see her lovely face light up.

Her eyes glistened. "Silly nut!"

THE SEA YIELDS treasures we least expect. Today Mark Twain washed up on the beach. I put the limp book on the oven door to dry, and tonight I looked at its contents. I am afraid, my dear Mark (or should I say, Sam?), I wouldn't trade your *Life on the Mississippi* or all the riverboats in the world for the shores of my island. Away from the sea, I would wither and perish like a jellyfish on dry land. It's the ultimate reality, the sea. It spawned life, and it extends life in me. I love its ebb and flow, its tang and its glitter, its anger and its calm, its mystery and boundless life. In comparison, lakes and rivers are fool's gold. As it girdles the island, the sea surrounds my life. I am either by it or on it, near it or in it. The salt chuck is not only food, fuel, and fertilizer, but it is our doorstep, company, and rummage room. It moderates the climate, presents gifts, and puts out fires. It's our foamy moat, highway, and swimming pool, lumberyard and tranquilizer, a source of exhilaration and freedom. And to my heart, a second home.

There are as many degrees of happiness as turns to a brook. Is the Mexican peon any happier in his simple existence

PICKING UP BEACH WOOD

than the city man, whose life is more complex? Life is the window from which each of us sees a different picture. What is my delight may well be another man's hell. Whether a river flows in front of our door, or the tide, we are happiest where *we* flow freely and strongly; where we continue to grow as we grow old.

JEANNE SAW the first hummingbird. The news completely upset the morning. "Where are the feeders?" she exclaimed,

BEACHCOMBING AT LOW TIDE

bursting into the room. "Hurry! Help me find them before he gets away."

Scholarly life has no appeal for me. The day bravely lived holds more truth than any book. I gravitate toward the axe or hoe, or the trail, more than to a chair. It is on my feet that my mind begins to soar. I must record my thoughts on the wing; too much study might ground them.

THE APPLE TREES are in bloom. What a heady scent! But it is the wild apples that have the loveliest blossoms.

All of this land was once an orchard, planted back in the nineties by Jack Chivers, the island's first owner. We have much for which to thank him—thirty apple trees, nearly a dozen pear trees, several plum trees, and the five-acre meadow as well. I have often thought how much he must have loved the island, for he spent the last twenty-eight years of his life here alone.

FOR WEEKS NOW I have had no inclination to leave the island. If I don't watch out, I'll soon take root like a fir. The prospect, I admit, I find not unpleasant.

THE MINK were at it again last night. We couldn't tell whether they were fighting or mating. The savage yipping and commotion in the bush are alike. They are not sociable creatures —even among their own kind. Their tempers are matched only by their viciousness. When two wandering males meet, the cove shudders. Nor do those who share the cove with us take kindly to our tenancy. A coexistence pact enables us both to live—if not quietly—at least peacefully.

The scrapper that lives below the house is an incorrigible gourmet. This morning he surfaced with a crab so large that we couldn't see his face. He slithered ashore, only to find his mouthful—once loose—too much to tackle on land. Nothing is less vulnerable than a giant crab backed against the rocks. When the mink slinked away in disgust, Jeanne pounced on the crab. "If he's not going to eat it, we will."

However, we are infuriated by the mink's housekeeping habits. They are grossly untidy, and a disturbing lack of the sense of smell makes them immune to the necessity of disposing of their garbage. Decayed crabs and fish carcasses reek from the floats where they use the logs as dinner tables. But

THE "GOURMET" MINK

what really maddens us is their making a dining room of the launch. "You know," Jeanne declared after the last mess, "I really need a fur coat."

THIS MORNING I awakened as if in a dream. The heavenly silence—so still my heart sounded like a drum. What perfect peace! In the city I remember sleep broken by the rumble and roar of traffic. Here, I awake to the stillness of the sun rays, the distant call of the eagle, the sea gently lapping the rocks. How many persons are as fortunate? My lot seems so much better than that of most men, it makes me wonder if something greater will be asked of me.

Tonight Davey put up quite a fuss in the tub. He objected to being scrubbed under his arms. A question of manliness—Davey insisted it was hair. "Just dirt," said Jeanne. "Look! It came off, didn't it?"
He burst into tears.

Our neighbor on Salt Spring, Dr. Mac, has a house—a showplace of old treasures, china, paintings, cut glass, and coins. Yet today, what did he show us first—his Vermeer, his Roman coins, or Crown Derby? No, the little guest cottage that he built with his own hands. He even knocked on the walls to show their sturdiness and pointed to the roof shakes he had split himself. This is his real treasure.

IT HAS BEEN a laborious day of weeding, pruning, and hacking salal back from lawns and trails. The growth is staggering. Relax a moment and the forest engulfs you. I really love the wild greenness, but the soul calls for order, and I must obey its demands. Then Jeanne is most articulate. "Those baby firs" —she points—"they'll be man-size in no time if we don't yank them out." An island never lets you rest. Your toehold is slippery. You're always about to be pushed into the sea. Nature works twenty-four hours a day. You, weary little man, must rest.

My writing is at a standstill. Chapter 5—Funny Wooden Blocks—is not quite right. Why is it I am finding it harder to get out of the well on paper than to get out physically when I fell in?

ENTRANCED! I am absorbed in the world of Emily Carr: her

art, her writings, her person. What I love is her courage and the incredible faith she had in her work that carried her through decades of study, striving, and anonymity. What is assigned to inspiration or sheer talent more deservedly belongs to sweat. The inner struggle that lay behind her creations is as enthralling as any canvas she ever painted. How she yearned to capture the spirit of the British Columbian forest! "What is that vital thing the woods contain, possess, that you want?" she writes in her *Journal.* "Why do you go back and back to the woods unsatisfied?" Her trips by trailer, surrounded by her animal friends, were not in vain. Even her first attempts were magnificent failures. Would that she had bequeathed me her spirit!

Nothing excites me as much as talent, whether it be in casting a fly or digging a ditch, in a boxer's left jab or a truth well skewered.

I love fishing, especially when I land a good thought.

JEANNE COMPLAINS that I am too soft-spoken—a nice way of saying I don't assert myself enough. This is true, I admit. With people, I am a genial apparition—more seen than heard. A bad egg at a restaurant refuses to rile me. I will not complain to the management. I just never go there again, and make sure to refer my friends to other places. If I were more dynamic, I would give radio broadcasts or go on lecture tours with what I wish to say. Instead, I find that I can express myself only from the apartness of my island and the silence of my den. That I am shy and lack assertion does not bother me. I'd rather saunter through life, dropping my apple seed, than try to bombard an audience with it from a podium.

In the garden, little lines of vegetables now—like soldiers —ready for an attack of weeds.

*

As we drove into Ganges this morning, the right fender fell off and rolled into a ditch. I stuck it disgustedly in the turtleback and in the village asked Lloyd at the garage to put it back on.

When the car was ready, Lloyd said, "Wouldn't drive too fast, folks. Only things holding them others on is mud."

By the time we reached Fernwood the fog was so thick we couldn't see the island.

"Let's hurry," Jeanne fretted, "before it gets any worse."

We cast off and bravely headed out with our fingers crossed, hoping we could hit Wallace and then follow shore to the cove. As the blank gray world enveloped the boat, I felt a little more jittery than usual. We have traversed the channel before in the fog, but this time we had Davey aboard and we couldn't afford to have anything happen.

"Aren't we going too far to the left?" Jeanne asked unsailorishly.

"Nope," I replied. "We're dead on course."

I looked at my watch. At 1500 rpm's the trip took only seven minutes.

The fog darkened. Only the weeping grayness was visible beyond the bow. A shape slid by the starboard side—a log—barely missing the hull. Wide-eyed, Davey peered ahead as Jeanne nervously lit a cigarette. Moments stretched into minutes.

"Think we've missed the island, Dave?"

I glanced again at the time. "Afraid so. We should have picked up shore a minute ago."

"What'll we do?" she gulped.

"Better get on the bow and watch for rocks." I slackened the throttle, feeling a pang of fear I didn't want to show.

"Say, Davey," I said, "how does a fly land on the ceiling?"

His worried expression turned to one of disgust.

"He doesn't, silly. He crawls up the wall."

Suddenly the gray void parted, revealing a fortress of

towering trees wreathed in white gauze. It was like some far-off country.

"Bottom!" Jeanne yelled. "You'd better stop."

Beneath us rocks loomed from the depths like the spine of a huge sea monster. I cut off the engine and scrambled to the bow. A hundred yards off, the mysterious shoreline lingered in the mist.

"Can't make out where we are, can you?"

"It's not Wallace—that's for sure." My eyes searched for some familiar clue. "Lord knows where we are."

Davey poked his head out the window. "Maybe it's where Alice lives." (We had been reading the famous classic to him.)

We grinned. As the tide swung us closer, the faint outline of a boathouse began to take shape.

"It's Dr. Mac's," Jeanne cried. "We've circled back and hit Salt Spring." She turned with a roguish smile. "You're some navigator, you are."

She was right, of course. But it made me wonder— the compass had never been wrong before. We retreated to the cabin, where I started to make an inspection. Then I saw it: Jeanne's handbag, next to the compass.

"Here's the culprit." I tossed it to her. "Enough metal in there to throw an ocean liner off course."

The fog seemed thinner and brighter. I took a fresh bearing and motioned Davey to sit on my lap.

"Okay, big boy, let's see if you can find Wallace."

THE FIRST WEEK of May brought many inquires but few reservations. Why? The letters I have not written; the glories of the island I have not proclaimed. Mr. Pichel wants to know the exact size of Wallace. Water temperature? Number of guests? Heat? Nearest doctor? Poison ivy? Is there a bridge? Golf? Maid service? What time is dinner served? The poor fellow! Wallace is not for him. How fearful one must be to leave nothing to chance.

AIRVIEW OF THE COVE

SCRUBBING THE *Islander*

I FEEL LIKE a pent-up animal here in the den. The cove shimmers like a story-book lagoon asleep in the woods, and the joyful cries of gulls reverberate in the shine and dazzle. I can't keep my eyes inside. No wonder literary master-pieces are more likely to be hatched in a dark, dingy room.

This afternoon I was routed from the workshop. "Dave!" Jeanne called. "Somebody's on the point. Come quick."

A small gray boat had pulled up opposite the house, and several men armed with what looked like mops and buckets were swarming over the rocky point.

"What do you make of it?" Jeanne asked.

I couldn't believe my eyes.

"They're painting the rocks—the crazy fools!" And I rushed down the bank.

"Stop it!" I shouted. "What in hell are you doing?"

Not a man raised his head. They continued to splash paint all over the rocks. The launch came toward me, and a ruddy-faced man stepped from the cockpit. "Government surveyors, sir," he said with a friendly smile. "We're making a new hydrographic chart of the islands."

I began to simmer down. "Do you have to ruin the point?"

"It's only whitewash." His tone was reassuring. "We've got to have a fix for the triangulation between shores."

When I reached the house, Jeanne said, "Well, of all things. What a funny way to make a chart."

I was nonplussed. "Didn't know anything was wrong with the present one."

IT IS DIFFICULT to do much writing now. I have made a rule: mornings in the den, rest of the day to the resort. What a stack of mail to answer! I am beginning to realize that the first requirement of a resort man is salesmanship. I must write a dozen letters to land one guest. The biggest stumbling blocks are women; they want meals. "I don't blame them," Jeanne says. "Who wants to cook on a vacation?"

Still, we are convinced there are enough people who want an "island" vacation and are willing to cook for themselves. How does one reach them? Do some brave males still hold the reins? Perhaps we should try the *Wall Street Journal*.

THIS MORNING I should have stayed in bed. The end float has sunk, the boats aren't painted, the honeymoon cottage leaks, and guests arrive June 2—less than two weeks away. Besides all this, the motor in the launch sounds sick. Which should I tend first? "You'd better fix the launch," Jeanne answered for me. "Else you won't have any supper tonight."

At tea just before bedtime, tired and depressed, I toyed with an idea. On an envelope I wrote: "Island for sale—200 acres, north of Victoria, B.C. Five housekeeping cottages and store. Orchard, wharf, and 8 small boats. Owner's cottage overlooks landlocked cove. Willing to trade for . . ." My pen stopped. I crumpled the paper and stepped outside. The air was heavy with the scent of honeysuckle and the stars glowed like spotlights in the sky. I felt an arm link mine, a voice say, "Darling, you can't see *this* in the city."

BLISTERY HOT. This has been the third week without rain. The forest is tinder dry—even the rugged salal droops from thirst. We've posted No Trespassing signs around the island. A negligent campfire, back in the twenties, burned off Wallace, and we don't wish it to happen again. Signs and constant patrolling are our only insurance.

After a morning of emptying my thoughts into the "machine," I love to dig in the garden. It fills me up again. I find the mind responds best when the muscles are toned and the blood warm in the veins. As the hoe bites the ground, my thoughts are weeded as well. "It's the best method,"

Thoreau declared, "to remove palaver out of one's style." Unfortunately, palaver is necessary to the resort man, but a menace to the creative man. How can a writer be original if he is not sincere?

To love gardening is to spoil half of one's boredom.

WHEW! The thermometer hit eighty at noon, but it's hotter inside than out. We ate lunch under the maples; barbecued salmon on the beach tonight. Why does food always taste better outdoors? "I know one thing," Jeanne said as we packed in the dishes. "It certainly doesn't pay. You and Davey eat twice as much."

The past few nights I have been reading David Grayson's *Adventures in Contentment* with great interest, and wondering why he's remained obscure. Now that I have finished, I realize he's pollyannish. All too tame and condescending. The inevitable consequence of a "public" personality triumphing over the "private" one. What author is not diminished by overexposure to public life? This has been the case with Hemingway, Mailer, Capote, and many others. For, as Cyril Connolly, the astute literary critic, remarked, "Ultimately, the public figure devours the private one." Is this not, I wonder, a lesson for me?

To be remembered: What I write must serve to mold me. How else can I catch up with the man that craves to be?

I HATE TO CONFESS it, but the healthiest-looking plant in the garden is chickweed. I am no farmer, hard as I try. Perhaps it's because my mind wanders that the carrots are spindly and the lettuce refuses to head. More likely, it's because I really prefer to farm for beauty rather than utility. Nothing thrills me as much as my coral begonia's first bloom. It gives me nourishment that carrots and spinach fail to provide.

BEGONIAS THRIVE IN THE FLOWER BOX

Likewise, I find quiet joy in watching a peace rose unfold its golden petals. However, to see a person burst into creative flower—that, to me, is the most beautiful sight of all.

Human life is my secret garden. I delight in extracting from each person I know all the perfection and beauty he holds. To abet and make known some verve, some ardor, some promise, fills all my quiet hours. People teem with talent, with hidden skills. It is only the lack of volition that keeps the bricklayer from building paragraphs rather than a wall. I hate to see a person marking time, who is not all he could be. What a waste of life! Without stretching, how does the fir cone take root? So with us, it's not so much our I.Q. that counts but our "I will." For no human plant is so barren that love cannot make fertile and ardor make it bloom.

My neighbor, Cecil Rollins, failed at everything. He tried to farm, to log, to fish. He couldn't eke out a bare existence for his growing family. One day I ran into him in Ganges. He had the look of a beaten man, though still in his early thirties. It took only a few minutes to discover his one great love—Salt Spring Island. He knew and worshipped every foot of it.

"Have you ever thought about selling property?" I asked.

He shrugged. "I can't sell anything. I'm used to working with these." He held out his huge rough hands.

"Have you tried?"

"Nope."

"Then how do you know you can't?" A man is never a failure who is unafraid of being one.

I called on the local realtor. He was short-staffed and needed a salesman, and he promised to talk to Cecil.

A month later, when I went over to Salt Spring after the mail, I never saw a happier, more prosperous-looking chap than Cecil Rollins, showing a city couple a waterfront lot.

Another time I found a girl disconsolately painting wing-tips in an aircraft plant. She wore dirty overalls, a bandana round her hair, and her face was pocked with paint—yet she was so beautiful, I stopped and stared. It seemed to jar every reasonable sense that she should be in such a noisy bedlam. I was an air force photographer on assignment. During lunch hour, she consented to a few portraits.

"Am I really photogenic?" she asked shyly. "You see, I've always wanted to be an actress. It's a dream of mine."

The photos exceeded my expectations. I was as excited, as was she. I persuaded her to quit her job and take up modeling, promised to teach her all I knew and introduce her to other photographers. Once she had made a few magazine covers, the studios would notice her. But my time was short; I was shipped overseas and lost track of her. A few years later, my paint-pocked beauty became a well known Hollywood actress—Marilyn Monroe.

Photography again helped in my quest.

I was taking a night school course in photogrammetry. Next to me sat a young man in his early twenties, with coal-black hair and dark, deep-set eyes. He was a hospital orderly by day, an amateur sculptor at night. Would I come to see his work? His basement room was like a Left Bank garret. Figurines, clay casts, statues, and busts filled the room. I was deeply impressed by his creations, the work of an extraordinary talent. How could he sell his sculpture, he asked. He was intensely shy, too embarrassed to invite anyone important in, and his pieces were too bulky to pack around on a bus.

"I'll photograph them," I said.

"I have no money."

"Doesn't matter. I've never done this before. It'll be good experience."

With a portfolio of prints, he persuaded bookstores and art shops he knew to exhibit his work. My seventy-five dollar DeSoto provided the transportation. In no time, he made sales. Art galleries began to take his sculpture. Shortly thereafter, he won a scholarship to a famous art academy. Today, Lowell Grant is a well-known children's sculptor whose hilltop studio overlooking Los Angeles is the envy of every artist with a dream.

A MAY MORNING is like waking inside a diamond. The world is a-glint and a-gleam. The Holland farmhouse on Salt Spring seems only a block away instead of a mile. Colored beads of wash hang from the Loiselle clothesline. Along the beach road, a car scurries among the trees—a black Volvo. Lloyd is off for work. As the dust settles, I see Dr. Mac digging in the garden, and down the road, Colonel Bailey hauling his boat up the beach.

We don't always have to *see* what our neighbors are doing. Yesterday the brisk westerly brought the yeasty aroma of fresh homemade bread. "The Hollands, I bet," Jeanne pinpointed the source. "Nellie loves to bake on windy days." Later came the unpleasant scent we readily recognized when Mr. Holland forked manure. The chatter of a chain saw reveals who is short of firewood; the thumping of a drilling machine, who is short of water. By the racket the cows make at milking time, we know Vic is napping—and when the Colonel comes home from fishing, by his vociferous oaths we know that he was skunked.

Salters are curious about us, too. Binoculars sit by every kitchen window. They let us know about the strange boat that lingers alongshore, who has been trespassing, and if we have injured or trapped sheep. All this proves helpful, particularly in summer when there's the constant danger of fire, and in winter, when poachers are after the mink.

Regrettably, we are often nuisances. Guests who arrive unexpectedly go down the road and honk—invariably in front of a house—and soon its occupant comes out in wrath. "What the devil are you doing? . . . Oh, it's the Conovers you're after. Better go down the road. Too many trees. They can't hear you here." Soon neighbors are shuffling cars back and forth, cursing, and wishing we had keener ears.

However, we get just as exasperated at them. Often their little fishing boats are stranded here by rough seas or motor trouble. It means either putting them up, fiddling with a cranky outboard, or taking them home. We don't mind being interrupted by genuine emergencies, but one old rascal's motor has the habit of conking out in front of the cove. Alfie says that he loves the island: "Yes, siree—the most beautiful spot on earth." But I think it is Jeanne he adores, for he always comes

ALFIE

up the path bearing cucumbers or squash—her favorite vegetables. This paves his approach to the living room sofa.

With all the exuberance his tall, fragile body can muster, he offers his gifts—"Somethin' from the garden, lassie."

Jeanne's smile makes any ordeal worthwhile. She's warm and wonderful with older people, far more patient with them than I am.

"Have you time for a cup of tea?"

Alfie's eyes brighten.

"Why, yes—I think so."

Afterward, it's a game of crib or a wander in the garden —the familiar "ohs" and "ahs," and I'm the one who's stuck with hauling him home in the dark.

WHOOPEE! The reservation chart is full. We're booked right through Labor Day.

WHEN WALLIE GOES sailing with Davey, his huge shaggy head is like a bronze figurehead on the dinghy. In any stance or repose, a collie is a beautiful creature. How he graces a lovely lawn! Our Wallie (short for Wallace) is incapable of being ungraceful, even when he hoists a leg. A Scotsman that takes to island living and to boats, he is a combination of gentleness and dignity, of lion and housecat—pure nobility, cinnamon and white with streaks of black, but he serves no useful purpose execpt to look the aristocrat. Considering it undignified to kiss or lick your hand, Wallie merely offers a gentlemanly paw. He likes to chase anything that moves, loves to trap mink in the rocks (his snout is battle scarred), and will ride the bow of the launch in a mountainous sea—yet a gunshot will find him cowering under the bed.

Wallie and I are as close as two males can be—we understand each other. As I write, he is looking up at me with wistful eyes, longing—as I am—to take to the woods. He is my shadow and mirror, reflecting my every mood. He settles peacefully at my feet even though I am spiritually off somewhere else. This is not disconcerting to *him*. But no human being likes to converse—let alone live—with a person who is not "all there!"

For fifteen years or so, Jeanne has grown used to my physical presence, but she has not grown used to my ambiguous ways. Her complaint—and it's well founded, I confess—

WALLIE

is that I belong less to her than I do to a rival—one whom, notwithstanding all her own considerable charms, she is unable to match. The world, she says, has stolen me from her. Even deprived me of myself. She is right, of course, for I find the day so filled with varied delights I am rarely conscious of time, my torn pants, the fact that I need a shave, or that I am tired or cold—even that I require a bath. We have an unspoken contract. She minds the body while I look after the soul.

We are alike only as two fluids. I am a river; she is a brook. She's clear—tinkles and rushes. I'm murky—quiet and ponderous. It is a source of continual wonder to me that our great differences could form so great a bond.

FOR SEVERAL DAYS we have been unpacking store stock, pricing and putting canned goods on the shelves. Jeanne is storekeeper. She has a liking for this sort of thing. But I find it time consuming and wearying, with little reward other than financial profit. *My* delight is in the profit I find in the customer rather than that which I take from the till.

I am amused by the ingenuity of manufacturers. The plugs and wobblers we have on display are designed to catch people more than fish.

MAY 24—THE TENTH YEAR on Wallace. I have come to this conclusion: Here where my heart dwells, so will my grave be. How wrong I was to think I could ever desert the island for the safer shores of society. For what I would lose in the trade I value far more highly than what society is able to offer. To exchange a boat for a car, for instance, is to give up adventure and freedom for a congested freeway where each day the scenery and destination never vary. In a boat I stand at the tiller, but who stands at his own helm among men? We live on the tide. Few men are self-driven; most, world-driven. As Chamfort said, "To be in one's hand, to be one's own man in heart and principle and feeling—that is the rarest thing." How everything occupies us except ourselves!

The older I grow, the more clearly I see the faults of society, the more I am inclined to live not as a recluse or misanthrope, but as a solitary man here on the fringe. I thrive best on my own soil, though another man may root better in society. I find the city a feast to the eye and to the glacial reign of the intellect, but so little there is to nourish the heart and spirit.

Self-service stores are empty of self-served man. Everyone wears, as Emerson put it, the "shopman's smile." The poverty of sincerity is so rampant that nothing is as rare as an authentic soul. Everything is show. Pursuit. A blur of busyness. The days merely business deals; the hours are but details, to be hurriedly wrapped up. It takes time to love. To be kind, to be *human*. Streetbound, I fear I would suffer a far greater malnutrition than if I were stranded on an island.

What makes the solitary life enjoyable is one's enthusiasms. Like the bear who lives on his winter fat, one actually lives on stored yearnings. For the moment is never so poor the heart cannot make rich. "I feel," as Henry Miller wrote to Anaïs Nin, "as though it would require years of isolation to exhaust my present richness."

I SHOULD HAVE known something was up by the seagull cries. But I was too interested in beaching the launch so that I could copper its bottom, to note the sky. It was close to high tide. The keel had just commenced to settle on the grid, and I was cutting props and placing them against the gunnel to keep the boat upright when the tide went out.

Suddenly the squall struck. Whitecaps began to pour through the gap straight for the boat. As waves lashed her sides, I grabbed the pike pole and fended her off the beach. My heart beat wildly. What to do? She'd pound herself to pieces. I called to Jeanne. "Get me some rope, hurry!" I yelled. The waves leaped higher. I could no longer keep the keel from thumping on the beach.

Jeanne ran up with the rope.

"Tie it to the bowline. I'll go and throw out the anchor. We'll try to pull her out." The *Islander* is a heavy lady—a twenty-two-foot clinker that grosses over a ton.

Hurriedly I climbed aboard, and grabbing the Northill, flung it with all my strength into the sea. The rope burned as it raced through my fingers. For a second I waited, then began to pull. Spume plastered my shirt to my skin, and my eyes smarted. Suddenly the rope slackened. "There's not enough scope," I shouted as the anchor came toward me. "I'll have to take it out farther." Jeanne was helpless. The boat had now swung broadside, shuddering as it banged the bottom.

The next instant, I was swimming, clutching the anchor in my hand. It weighed only twelve pounds, but it felt more like fifty. Waves engulfed me—I gasped for breath, could barely see. A hundred feet seemed like an eternity. As I dropped the anchor, I saw Jeanne's figure on the stern. Before I reached the beach, she had the boat free and clear.

We lay on the sand and rested. Jeanne turned with a timid smile. "Nothing comes easy on an island, does it?"

I COULD NOT give myself wholeheartedly to any specialty—say architecture, for instance—for no matter how deep I pry or study, I find only facts and figures and so little of humanity. It is the structure of man that interests me, the inner symmetry of fine souls. Any specialty, in the long run, drives me from him.

It always comes as a shock how much we have to learn in order to know what to forget.

WE'VE BEEN PICKING wild strawberries before guests arrive. They are thick among the salal on the road to Pebble Beach. While we filled our pots, crows screamed at every berry, mad because they had missed so many. The blackberries are still green, but by the size of the crop, the guests will soon have a feast along with the crows.

We often wish we were more self sufficient, but the resort precludes that possibility. We buy a great deal of our food. Nowadays people want frozen—not fresh—vegetables. They want pasteurized, fortified, homogenized milk—not the delectable nectar that comes from Vic's cows. We've even given up chickens, which didn't mix well with guests. However, we do enjoy the island's bounty. Thanks to the warm spring, we have already sampled rhubarb, lettuce, and carrots from our own soil. The root cellar holds last year's crops—apples, potatoes, and squash. The shelves are packed with jams, bottled berries, pears, and plums. Besides peas, pickles, and tomatoes. For entrees, we have a choice of fresh lamb or mutton, salmon or cod. And, tides permitting—though we are none too fond of either—oysters and clams. A token self-sufficiency, but it gives us a wealthy feeling, and if I am not mistaken, adds a little earthiness to the soarings of the mind.

Spirea is in bloom. Of all nature's displays, spirea or "ocean spray" is our favorite bush. Its pendulous branches form an arbor of golden plumes over every trail—a mass of starlike whorls that evade description as each season their beauty evades my camera.

"IF THERE IS MAGIC on this planet," Loren Eiseley says, "it is contained in water." I am inclined to agree with him. This morning as I entered the workshop, my eye caught the bucket of rainwater. It was alive with wigglers where yesterday there apparently were none. I stopped to marvel at the emergence of life from nothing. That these black squirmers would soon be mosquitoes to make our life miserable did not alter the fact that I had witnessed a miracle.

How ephemeral facts are!

Time laughs at man's certainties. For every age leaves behind a wastepile of broken bits of knowledge—theories and beliefs once thought to be rock-firm. The great epoch-makers were fact-busters—Galileo, Columbus, Darwin, Freud, and others—who, ignoring the old facts, established new ones. What we consider a "fact" resembles an invention; no sooner is it perfected than it is replaced by another. Knowledge is partial; the facts are never "all in." The Piltdown man lurks beneath every boulder, just as every saint arrives clothed as a heretic. Now, this century's saint—Einstein—is being questioned. But alas—I have long since lost my faith in facts. "I'm certain of nothing," said Keats, "but the holiness of the heart's affections." Facts not proven in books, but proven by the pulse. I now believe in more concrete things: the power of prayer, the miracle of a begonia tuber, the infinity in every man, the morning greeting my collie will give me, and that with the certainty of fall, the bandtail pigeons will return to devour the berries in the madrona trees.

IT'S NEARLY JUNE and we are sprucing up for guests. Wallie has had a scrubbing in the tub (along with Davey), the windows are washed, and the garbage can is hidden behind the shed. In the closet, Jeanne's freshly ironed blouses hang next to suntans that have the clean smell of bleach. Fingernails are clean and cut, hair cropped and groomed. We are about to shed our private lives for public ones, as the countryman does when he visits the city. From winter's introspection and indoor life, we are prepared to flow outward, become less selfish and more generous. Summer is a social affair.

"We're ready," Jeanne declared after an inspection of the cottages. "Bring on the invasion."

It is paradoxical that as soon as man rushed into the cities, he began to think of ways to escape them. Now that summer stirs in his bones, he's ready to move outdoors to renew his heritage by joining "the greatest of all communities," as Joseph Wood Krutch observed, "which shares with us the great adventure of being alive."

Summer

We are all tourists really,
discovering new regions in ourselves and
in others.

—Gilean Douglas

A Lazy Summer Afternoon

THE BARBARIANS have arrived with their diving gear, tackle boxes, cameras, suntan lotions, outboard motors, ice chests, hair driers, portable barbecues, and walkie-talkies.

They look all alike—eager, tired, and pale—but soon fall into two types: the "rusher," who tries to do everything the moment he arrives, and the "sluggard," who is our favorite. He staggers into the yard mumbling that he is not to be disturbed, and falls into a hammock-coma that lasts the duration of his stay.

We can tell the rusher in advance. Invariably American, he comes loaded with golf clubs, baseballs, tennis racquets, scuba gear, and medicine balls. He dashes first for the shuffleboard, then badminton, then off for a swim. This merely winds him up. With a highball tinkling in one hand, he pitches horseshoes and darts, then rushes off for a five-mile hike. He knocks constantly at the door for us to play volleyball or take him water skiing and badgers us for bridge or canasta at night. By Labor Day, he leaves us so exhausted we feel like outlawing the human race from our shores.

It took us a long time to learn the realistic approach.

Busy Day at the Wharf

Guests do not need pampering. We just point out things to do (and *not* to do), and the island does the rest.

Now, when we spot a baseball bat or a snorkel, we are prepared. "Oysters are to the left of the wharf," we say, "clam beds on the right at the far end of the cove." Nothing slows a man down like a diet of shellfish. The digging, of course, helps as much as anything. The happy hour—the predinner drink that turns into an evening affair—we've learned to avoid. No one likes to see the manager drunk. And when you're a bit tipsy nothing is harder to fix than a generator when the lights go out.

THE RICHES are here again. She is pretty, matronly, a chatterer, and as disorganized as her noisy moppets. Henry is short, serious, and fortyish—a quiet man with thinning gray hair and a craggy face that reminds one of a professor. He has lost some of his shyness and looks ten years younger, as if in the course of winter he had taken on a mistress.

"Why, he even laughs," said Jeanne. "What's come over him?"

"It's his new job," I replied. "Remember the San Jose newspaper column he sent—'Roaming with Rich'? Maybe it's given him a lift."

I remembered the evening we were at Porlier Pass. The rods were out, the sky was crimson, and herring were arcs of silver on the surface. It was our third night. I felt relaxed with Henry. He didn't say much and seemed to enjoy himself—unlike most guests—without the urgent necessity of catching anything except perhaps a glimpse of a school of blackfish or an Indian lad hoisting a struggling salmon into his canoe. As I glanced at him, his eyes were darker and more distant than usual. His expression was not that of a successful magazine writer, but of a troubled man.

"Dave, I don't know why," he began. "My stories seem to drop from sight. People forget them. Nope, I don't get it,

Dave. I'm right at the top, next to O'Hara in the *Post*. Yet critics ignore me."

He lit a cigarette shakily. "It's no good. Stories get harder and harder to grind out. You've read them. They're good and solid, Dave. Why aren't they recognized?"

My heart went out to him. I knew the trouble—at least, I thought I did.

"Perhaps your aim is too high, Henry," I said softly. "You just haven't found your niche. You were a reporter. Isn't it possible journalism is more your meat?"

"How could it be?" he exclaimed. "I sell to the top magazines month after month."

"Weren't you happier as a newspaperman?"

He thought.

"Yes, I suppose so."

"Well, then, why not switch? The pay might not be so good, but the satisfaction might be twice as great."

I have often wondered why Henry failed to win literary recognition. Much as I liked him—his gentleness and self-effacing manner—I believe he lacked personal voltage, the inner spark that permeates a subject, lights up a yarn, and makes it glow in memory. Vital art is not the product of purely technical virtuosity. It is first and foremost the expression of a unique personality. We can forgive sloppy craftsmanship, overlook a writer's morals, disagree heartily with what he says, but we cannot tolerate dullness.

WRETCHED PEOPLE! This evening Mr. Snell was not satisfied that he caught four salmon and six grilse. When we got home, he expected me to clean and wrap them as well. What ignobility hides behind the word *sportsman!*

I am not, I admit, a good resort man. I forget to shave, can't remember names, lack talent and inclination for small talk, and I'm ill at ease in a group. Those who have no spine or purpose beyond their own private gain do not interest me. I would sooner follow the course of a butterfly through the woods than a spiel on the course of the stock market. . . . I quickly latch onto the person who has found something in his life greater than himself. Such people make me believe there is a natural aristocracy among men as surely as there is a hierarchy among animals.

LAST NIGHT I fell asleep thinking that there is nothing we pay more for than money.

FREDDIE IS unquestionably the best router-outer in the world. At daybreak he dropped clamshells on the roof, then padded across the shingles. Squawk! Squawk!—and the whole resort was awake. Times like these make me wonder why I like crows. Actually, I think, it's because I feel sorry for them. How dreadful it must feel to be a bird and to be so unbirdlike. To have neither particular beauty nor graceful flight. To have no song—just a loud mouth. As a result, crows have become more attuned to the world of men. They are arrogant, mischievous, and crafty—qualities so human that they remind some people of themselves. However, I try to overlook their peculiarities like those of old friends, but I admit they are hard to love. Particularly Freddie, who drops garbage on the lawn, attacks groceries left in the boat, and spoils more apples than he eats.

Yet I admire his zest; he's alive from beak to toe tips, and so bold he thrives in the sights of a shotgun. "A creature"—as Keats said of a stoat—"with a purpose, and its eyes are bright with it." What man is so admirably tuned? Yes, a bird with a delicate sense of humor who enjoys a good "haw-haw!" even better than a raucous "caw!" But it's on the trail, when Freddie clicks his castanets from a lofty fir, I love him best of all.

Jeanne does not share my feelings. Anyone who robs her

larder robs her pocketbook. To her, Freddie is the ringleader of a band of crooks.

THE THERMOMETER hit ninety at noon—the warmest June that we can remember. Yet what does a guest do first when he arrives? Lights the fireplace. Man has drifted so far from his primitive origins that a wood fire is a novelty. Thank God, one instinct remains as strong as ever. When I was returning from the well this afternoon, did I not hear the sober Jason couple romping in the bush?

THOSE WITH the best dispositions make the best gardeners. I don't believe in the green thumb, luck, or extra work when it comes to flowers. Plants, like animals, respond to kindness —more properly, to a certain personal magnetism of which kindness plays only a part. The same thing holds true with fishing. Some men—hard as they try—can never catch a salmon. Others do, quite easily. For years, as a guide, I have seen this happen—in the same boat, with the same tackle. Invariably one will catch the fish. The other just comes along for the ride.

The theory of personal magnetism is not acceptable in this scientific age. We are more concerned with means than ends. We want facts and statistics. For my part, not really being a clever person, I rely on the senses as much as the brain. I am more propelled by what I *feel* I know than what the mind *thinks* it knows. Pascal once defined man as the "thinking reed." He was overly optimistic. The head has not solved the human predicament: the need of mankind to secure a harmonious and peaceful state. The true value of intelligence lies in the service of love. On the revival of the "heart" may well depend human destiny. As a wise soul said, "Logic makes a good servant but a poor master." What better proof is there than man?

VIC IS A PEACH. He rowed over this afternoon against the swift current to inform us someone had left their headlights on. His arms had good reason to feel—as he put it—"like they've been yanked from their sockets." A tumblerful of rye soon dispelled his misery.

Casualties: one window pane, three lost horseshoes, nine Ping-Pong balls, two broken oars, and one crab pot. The damn Jenkins kid!

THE ISLAND RESEMBLES a city with its many services and utilities that must be maintained without interruption. You are the storekeeper, plumber, electrician, garbage collector, taxi driver, and often the doctor—all rolled into one. You are also the fireman and watchman, the water, gas, and power companies, the telephone exchange, health officer and unofficial justice of the peace.

More often, an island is like a ship constantly at sea. As captain, you feel a deep responsibility for your twenty-six passengers. You mingle, point out the sights, and help plan their day. You settle arguments, head the complaints department, and lend a sympathetic ear to personal problems and every dilemma of the human psyche. You learn to forgive —even grow fond of testy Mrs. Chard, who threatened the water supply by doing three weeks' laundry; and Mr. Dane, who is seized with an insatiable desire to yak the moment he spies you. You sleep lightly (if you can), to awaken at the slightest cough of the generator. You find yourself prowling at all hours inspecting your ship. Fire out in the lounge? Is a tap running? Have the badminton racquets been put away? Did Mr. Morgan tie up the rowboat properly? Has someone left a light on?

Generating power offers many problems. We are restricted to two thousand watts—for lights only. When guests arrive, we are forced to put them through "customs."

"Do you have any appliances?"

Mrs. Kirby cried, "Don't you have electricity?"

We explain: "Not for toasters, percolators, irons, hair driers, and electric blankets."

But when we forget to ask—wow! The lights suddenly dim, the plant groans, emitting a metallic death rattle, and I dash for the workshop to shut it off. With a flashlight, I go from cottage to cottage—"What's wrong?" "What's happened to the lights?"—to find the hidden culprit. Someone has plugged in a heating pad, and we substitute a hot-water bottle. Once again, the island beams with light and merry faces.

JUNE 25: Thirty-five years old. Where in life—if one had the choice—should one stop the clock? What I would like is to stop life here, halfway between the past and the future, and enjoy forever the two-fold advantage of youth and age.

Jeanne stared at me.

"Let's get our facts straight. I told Mrs. Kirby the island was two miles long. You told her it was two and a half. Which is it?"

I blushed.

"Both—depends on the tide."

THE NERVE! A yacht is anchored in front of the house, so close we can see the stitches in the sail. In the cockpit a man sits glumly, glass in hand and radio blaring. He appears to be stuck here for the night. We wouldn't have minded had he gone down the cove a bit, but right before our eyes —well, it hurts.

This makes us pull our blinds, something only the extreme cold forces us to do.

"It's strange," Jeanne said. "I think people have grown afraid of privacy. So they spoil it for others."

In fact, they try to avoid its remote possibility. In Los Angeles I was always disturbed by the many undrawn windows at night through which any passerby could view family intimacies as if he were witnessing a grade B movie. There is some terrible emptiness in people who bare the pages of their lives like open books. It's doubtful whether they are worth reading. "The most interesting people are those about whom we continue to know least," said Elizabeth Bowen. "Not because they surround themselves in mystery, but because some unconscious dignity in them forbids intrusion, and modesty keeps them from easy confidence. To them, with their untold secrets, the imagination, fascinated, returns."

I AM AMUSED at how desperately Americans try to unwind. After ten days, Morgan and Roberts are still going full blast. They've broken two badminton racquets, lost three fishing lines, wrecked a bicycle, and turned the horseshoe pits into bomb craters. For an American, it seems, the simplest thing is the hardest to do: nothing.

How often energy is mistaken for enthusiasm!

We love poking fun at Americans. Perhaps it's because, as Jeanne says, "We've got an inside track. They don't know we are Americans, too."

MY FISHING SKILL vanishes when I take a friend out instead of a customer. It's as if salmon know when it pays to be caught! At Porlier Pass it proved a better evening for thought than for fish, though Vic did manage to hook a starfish. What a contrast his companionship makes to that of our American visitors! The silences are peaks of the evening. They reveal honey-colored madrona along the shore, seabirds wheeling overhead, and the moon dimpling the sea with a silver sheen.

CONTENTED GUESTS

OUR HOUSE

Our spirits converge and converse. With lawyers and stock-
brokers, the air is never free of the smog of chatter. I feel
deprived of both the night and myself—even control of the
boat in the swirling current. No serene landscape or wonder
disturbs their eternal buzzing. They blot out the sunset with
themselves, and I come home exhausted and impoverished.

"What a mess!" Jeanne exclaimed, visiting the workshop this morning. "Why don't you clean up this place?"

THE AUTHOR WITH A FORTY-SIX-POUND SALMON

Shavings littered the floor and the bench swarmed with tools.

She has said this before—she will say it again when she looks for the pruning clippers and oil can. And I will repeat, "If I did, how would I find anything?"

Besides, I dislike the immaculate workshop. Sawdust and clutter speak of activity. And life. Spotless saws, gleaming wrenches, the shiny hammer on the wall, speak of little use. Americans are by nature too tidy, too efficient, too methodical. Fortunes are made on patent medicines, so afraid are they of missing a bowel movement. I am trying to shed this overly civilized state. The tidiest and cleanest places I know are haunts of the dead—museums and funeral parlors.

MRS. FRALEY LOOKED at the library and shook her head.

"You have so many old books, Mr. Conover. Bacon . . . Shakespeare . . . Plato. Don't you find them boring?" Her eyes fell on the *Analects of Confucius*. "Now who would want to read that?"

I pointed to the fiction section and to the row of currently popular novels on the mantelpiece.

How easy it is to condemn a work beyond our own immediate appreciation. At Christmas a guest sent us a copy of *Cosmic Consciousness*. Horrors! I thought. A mass of babbling mysticism. It sat gathering dust for several months until one day I happened to be reading Overstreet's *Enduring Quest*. He explained the valuable contribution this book had made to man's understanding of himself. With more respect, I picked up *Cosmic Consciousness* and found it a fascinating voyage into a new world of thought.

WE WERE RAKING leaves when little Sammy Peters came running up the path. "Mr. Conover!" he shouted. "Mr. Conover, a boat is on the rocks!"

I grabbed his arm. "Where?"

"Panther Point." He was almost too excited to talk. "A sailboat . . . it's sinking."

I turned to Jeanne. "Knew the government should have marked that reef. This makes the fifth shipwreck. Hold down the fort, will you?" And I took off for the wharf.

Some of the guests must have heard the shouts. "Can I come along?" asked Jason as I got into the launch.

"Me, too." Morgan rushed up. "Can I come?"

"Can you swim?"

They nodded.

"Okay. I may need some help. Pile in," After the last rescue, when a guest nearly drowned, I wasn't taking any chances.

Nearing the point, we spotted the thirty-foot ketch hard aground on the reef that ran a quarter mile offshore. She had a forty-five-degree list, the starboard deck was awash, and her sails fluttered helplessly in the southeasterly swells. The skipper stood atop the cabin, waving.

"Least the passengers got off safely." Jason nodded toward a woman and two children on the point.

We pulled in closer to the ketch.

"Afraid I'll lose her if I don't get her off," the skipper cried. I knew he spoke the truth. The reef gripped her keel while the ship itself hung over the cliff side of the reef—and the tide was falling fast. "Can you help?" his voice rang out.

"We'll try," I called back. "Throw me a line."

It would be a tricky maneuver. She had been grounded too long to come off on a straight pull. The only chance was to yard her sideways, in a twisting motion, toward the shoals —with the hope she would slide off in deep water and right herself.

Jason caught the line. When it was secured, I opened the throttle and headed the bow in the direction of the reef. The rope tightened, the propeller thrashed. The launch pitched and tossed in the swells. Ahead waves surged and tumbled over half-exposed rocks. I was afraid that I could not remember the passageway, that the wind would . . .

"She's not moving," Morgan yelled. "Give her more gas."

The wind was pushing us toward the sailboat, its masts threatening to slam against the cabin. My hand shook as I poured on more throttle. But the burst of speed only worsened the noise and vibration. She wouldn't budge.

I glanced at the floundering craft. The skipper clung to the mizzen, his face desolate. My heart went heavy, for I sensed what it meant to him. She was no ordinary boat, but one undoubtedly built with his own hands.

Then it came to me.

"It might help," I shouted, "if we had weight on the masts."

He gestured approval and began to shinny himself out on the pitching mizzen.

"I'll help him," Jason said, "if we can get close enough."

"All right. It just might to do it. But *hang on!*" Then I pointed toward the lifejackets. "You'd better get into one of those."

We came abreast of the forward mast. It was barely six feet above the swells. I turned sharply. As it swung over the cockpit, Jason grabbed it and flung himself aboard. I pulled away slowly till the rope tightened—then gunned the throttle. The motor roared.

"That's doin' it," Morgan yelled. "Keep goin'."

We were slowly creeping ahead when the launch suddenly lurched. There were shouts. Over my shoulder I saw the masts shoot up in a spray of sea foam as the sailboat righted. Soaked and grinning, Jason and the skipper slid down to the decks and waved triumphantly.

This evening a knock came on the door.

"I'd like you to have this"—the skipper held out the ship's life ring, engraved in gold letters WAYFARER II—"as a token of gratitude from myself and the crew."

FOR SEVERAL DAYS Mr. Fraley has been looking for his dentures, which he lost while swimming. We helped, but finally concluded that a crab with a twisted sense of humor has taken possession and is now making quite a show of them.

July 4: Davey is disappointed. "No fireworks," I said to him. "Not with all these Canadians here."
Jeanne smiled. "Long live the Queen!"

A resort is like a farm. It depends on two variables: salmon and the weather. You can keep a Californian happy when the fishing is poor only if the weather is good. When both are poor, it's like a crop failure—he fails to come up next year.

WE WERE GOING OVER the store stock when Jeanne said, "You know, if Albert Merriweather wasn't so likeable, he'd be a pain in the neck. The poor man—he's just accident-prone." Jeanne is atrociously sympathetic to helpless males. They invariably bug her less than they do me.
I winced.
"If you ask me, he was an accident to begin with."
"Don't be silly, Dave. He can't help it. His blue eyes are as innocent as a schoolboy's. Besides, he apologizes, doesn't he?"
Jeanne could afford to be sympathetic. She wasn't around on his arrival when his suitcase ripped off the boat fire-extinguisher and shot carbon tet. in his eyes. Nor was she around the next afternoon when he approached sheepishly and said, "Mr. Conover, could I trouble you? My class ring . . . Well—it's down the basin trap." Or while I sweated a whole morning trying to repair a mangled fishing outfit he had left under the gangway when the tide came in.
It was Thursday that our worries really mounted. Albert wanted to rent a motorboat. I wasn't keen on the idea. But

some were idle—we couldn't very well refuse him. Jeanne gave me hope. "Maybe with his wife along he'll be more cautious." We fixed him up with reliable old *Bertha*, plenty of gas, and a chart that plainly marked every reef.

"Even if the passages look good," I warned him, "don't trust them. Play safe. Always go by the chart." He nodded with such sincerity that for a moment I thought I liked the guy.

Well, dinnertime came and no Albert. The sun fell behind the firs—still no sign. In the dark, we stood outdoors and listened for *Bertha*'s heartbeat. His friends the Carmichels drifted into the yard. We were all worried. The night was so quiet we could hear a leaf drop. Still not a sound. We thought of everything that could have happened. Had he fallen overboard? Was the boat on a . . . ?

"DAVE! Oh, D-A-V-E!" The shouts suddenly pierced the darkness.

We pointed the flash toward the entrance of the cove.

"That was Albert's voice," Jeanne exclaimed. "But I don't see the boat."

"Come on," I said. "Let's go look for him."

In the launch—equipped with a half-mile spotlight—we began to comb the channel. It wasn't long before the light picked up *Bertha* a hundred yards offshore. Pulling alongside, I said, "Are we glad to see you! What's wrong with the motor?"

Albert stood holding an oar. "Nothing." He shrugged good naturedly. "It goes but the boat doesn't move. So we had to paddle."

"And we've paddled for hours," added Mrs. Merriweather.

I thought this strange. After we returned and the Merriweathers had gone to their cottage, I inspected the boat. A ball of seaweed was knotted around the prop. No wonder *Bertha* wouldn't move.

The next morning I informed Albert.

"Seaweed!" he cried, astonished. "You mean I did all that paddling for nothing?" I nodded.

We agreed the trouble could have been worse—had a squall arisen—and the episode discouraged him from renting boats. Thenceforth, he decided that he would do all his fishing with me.

The following evening at Porlier Pass was one I wish not to remember. The sea was choppy, but the fish were biting. A big one hit the handline trolling from the stern. The safety rubber stretched twice its normal length—a sign of a twenty-pounder or better. Grabbing the line, Albert began quickly to pull it in.

"Not so fast," I cautioned. "Let him run a bit."

But Albert was excited. His hands kept yanking the fish closer to the boat. All of a sudden something parted, and the spoon flew out of the boiling water and struck his hand. Groaning, he clutched his palm in agony. The #9 hook, as large as a silver dollar, had penetrated the flesh shank-deep. He slumped on the seat, the blood streaming down his arm.

I hurried for the first-aid kit, drew out the sharp knife I kept for such an emergency, and prepared to cut the hook out. The boat rocked and rolled aimlessly as it wallowed in the boils.

"It's going to hurt," I said, bracing myself against the gunnel.

"Can't hurt worse than it does now," he muttered.

I dug the knife into his hand, cutting the flesh swiftly round the hook. He grimaced with pain as I withdrew it.

"Quick. Put your hand in the sea," I said. "It'll cleanse the wound."

When the bleeding had subsided, I bandaged his hand and we took off for Wallace.

In the morning we were greatly relieved. "I'd like to settle the bill," he said, coming into the store. "I think I'd better go home."

We couldn't have agreed with him more.

I AM THINKING how quick my friends are to retire. "Yes, I'm quitting the garage," said Lloyd the other day. "I'm tired of working on old hacks. I'm going to raise ponies and pigs. The ponies for love—the pigs for meat." He is just forty-five. Now I see him out fishing (Ella even cans the cod), and on clear days, bringing hay into the barn. How I admire these islanders! I no longer frown on their eccentricities. It takes a lot of talent to be content with little money.

When you stop and think, isn't success really *freedom* —living the life you want?

TINDER DRY. No rain has fallen since early May; the grass is burnt brown except under the apple trees, and the garden withers. Danger of fire worries us.

"How's the water?" Jeanne asked while collecting the shriveled beans.

"Not good," I said. "I've had to cut back the toilets. The well is dropping fast."

WHEN THE HORN sounded this afternoon, we knew it meant trouble. "Relatives, I bet," Jeanne said with psychic premonition. "The next guests aren't due till tomorrow."

Once the word gets around that you own and live on an island, it's something like winning the Irish Sweepstakes. It's amazing how many relatives suddenly spring up. Ones you never knew existed. My grandfather raised two families. Jeanne's grandparents had a dozen kids. They come without writing or phoning—usually by car—and, to the annoyance of neighbors, vigorously pound on their horns. Such was the case today.

While Jeanne tidied the house, I zipped over to see who it could be. Resembling a plump Gainsborough, an elderly lady came rushing down the gangway, holding onto a wide-brimmed hat, which flapped in the wind. Before I had my feet planted on the float, she flung her arms around me.

My God! I thought, whose relative is this—Jeanne's or mine?

She looked into my shocked eyes. "You don't remember your Aunt Peggy, do you?" Her Southern drawl was as thick as her perfume. "I took care of you when you were a wee one. You were such an imp. You used to throw tomatoes at passing cars. Of course, you wouldn't remember."

She stepped back and took a long look. "My, how you've grown. So big, tall, and handsome. How time flies." Turning to the nondescript man behind her, she said, "Dave, this is John. Isn't he a dear? The sweetest man you ever saw?" His limp hand shook mine.

"Tell me, is that your island?" Aunt Peggy pointed toward Wallace.

I nodded numbly.

"Oh, I can't wait to see it. We've come all the way from Kansas City. We've got loads of time. We want to see every inch."

I did not like the way she said "loads of time." Maybe she had, but we hadn't. My eyes caught the huge stack of luggage on the ramp. Good Lord—they were out to spend the summer with us! Nope, I wasn't going to be sucked in by this pair, even if she *had* put diapers on me.

"I'm sorry, Aunt Peggy. We're awfully busy. Besides, there's no room. . . . we're full up. I'll try to find accommodations for you at the Harbour House."

ANOTHER DAY in the nineties. This heat—it's easy on the woodpile but hell on water. We've put notices in the cottages: WATER IS PRECIOUS. PLEASE USE IT SPARINGLY. FLUSH TOILETS ONLY WHEN ABSOLUTELY NECESSARY.

Why, oh why, do little boys (and big ones) rush to a johnny when nature provides opportunity everywhere?

"I swear Mr. Fraley showers twice a day," I said to Jeanne. "His skin looks drier than parchment paper. Why do Americans have to bathe so often?"

Jeanne smiled. "Maybe it's because they're trying to purify themselves of their sins."

Americans remind me of the Romans. Their ritual of bathing, their obsession with the body, the millions spent annually on soaps, toothpaste, deodorants, sprays, and mouthwashes, all to assuage a mania for cleanliness. No other people in history have been so conscious of the way they look, smell, and feel. At times I wonder if this intense preoccupation with the flesh is not itself a detergent that dissolves the grit of human worth. As Sidney J. Harris put it so well, "It is infinitely easier to purify the breath than to purify the spirit," which reminds me—wasn't it the "care of the spirit" rather than the "cult of the body" that made ancient Greece outshine the glory of Rome?

Only in the country do we get to know the city dweller. Can it be true that only abroad we come to know our own countryman? It is when we cease to do the things we have to do, and do the things we like to do, that we are revealed in the truest light.

I WAS REPAIRING the runabout when Mr. Jones rushed down the gangway in a state of agitation. "The radio doesn't work —it's dead. Can you fix it? I've got to hear the twelve o'clock news."

I dropped my tools (muttering a silent oath), and took the battery set into the workshop. After I had it fixed, but couldn't get it back into the case, I exploded. News! News! Every day men die of it, little by little, for the lack of something new in themselves. For what else so readily fills the vacuum of our lives?

Yes, we do get keyed up. Life here depends on motors —generators, pumps, washers, lawn mowers, and boats. They run perfectly except when they are most needed. We get awfully rattled when they stop. But we don't need tranquilizers. We just hop in the skiff and row. This is our magic carpet from which we see the marine fairyland below, drifting marshmallow clouds above, and fir-clad islands all around. As the oars dip, the trees wiggle and stretch upon the surface. A kingfisher dives and dashes off with his breakfast. Along the sandstone ridge, a mink scurries with a squirming crab in his jaws. The scent of resinous cedar and the sea fills the lungs; the peace and wonder of it all soaks into the pores. The tension fades, the senses take over. Your strokes are slower now, deeper, more rhythmic. The heart has stopped its pounding. The sea against the planks is the murmur of many voices. Joy rushes into the soul. The world smiles with the brittle glitter of sunshine.

THIS MORNING Jeanne overheard Mrs. Barnes, while sitting on the edge of the sandbox, ask Davey, "What do you like to do best, son?"

"Fishin'."

"Second best?"

He thought for a second.

"Fishin' with Papa."

Deluged with yachts tonight—collected $13.50 in moorage. Must be thirty or forty people ashore, wandering about the yard, in the lounge, peeking in windows, playing shuffleboard, dropping candy wrappers everywhere. What a mob! We've had to hide the horseshoes and badminton racquets.

Guests have fled into their cottages. Quite a problem, but we do need the money.

"I'm thankful for one thing," Jeanne sighed. "They're only here for the night."

The sea jockeys have taken over the waterways. The old-time yachtsman of wealthy gentility and varnished wheelhouse has become a creature of the past. In a way, we regret his demise, for he was usually polite, appreciative, and quiet. He had a fondness for the sea and invariably traveled alone. Not so with outboard cruiser owners—sea jockeys, as we call them. They are boisterous, often ill-mannered, travel in packs, and are less intrigued by the sea than the swiftness with which they can skim over it. A destination is anywhere that can be made by nightfall; anything in between that slackens the throttle, an aggravation. In yachting clothes, they neither feel nor look the skipper, as they munch fat cigars and squash their vizored caps over their ears.

At home the "nouveau" yachtsman may not be the boss, but at sea he's Captain Bligh. "You numbskulls!" he shrieks at his family. "Trim the ship. Don't all stand on one side. . . . For God's sake, woman! Let me have the wheel. You're going to hit the dock." The blue denims and cap make him feel wealthy, the cigar makes him feel "big." But for the missus, squeezed into a cubicle not much larger than a telephone booth with a pack of restless kids, keeping a semblance of order and cooking three meals a day is seldom fun. As one wife confessed, "I'd rather be back at Boeing bucking rivets than go through this again."

I NOTE MRS. BARNES is reading *Rector of Justin* by Louis Auchincloss, the New York novelist whose work I greatly admire. His books are superbly created—yet why do they so frequently fail to satisfy? The quality they lack is not one of skill but rather of intensity, a certain blood-heat that gives them life. "He has everything necessary to create the essential art," said one perceptive critic, "except what is absolutely vital—passion." Perhaps, my dear Auchincloss, you should journey to Italy as Goethe did, to renew those vital juices eroded by public life.

All day I am ruled by a fierce tyrant, but at night my secret joy is to escape to paper; here I am in command. Safe from interruption, I canvas the day of thoughts, bank them in my journals so that at some future date they may accrue sufficient interest to yield a book.

GUESTS FREQUENTLY ASK, "Living here the year around, don't you ever get lonely? Or bored?" Frankly, we haven't given it much thought. When an island enters your life it's like a three-party marriage. You are so busy tending to one or the other, you rarely have time to think of yourself. Yes, to be sure, the first winters we experienced loneliness—and we still do—when parted for long from the island or from each other. But, ever since, we have been surprised at the increasing pleasure and satisfaction we find in our aloneness. Surprisingly, we have met more people and made more friends than would have been likely if we had remained in Los Angeles. One summer the guest book logged 340 prospective friends. Often the mail brings us closer to people than a coffee klatch or dinner party would. Loneliness is a funny thing. It is not the result, we found, of being cut off from people—but of being cut off from ourselves. Where is loneliness more intense than in the largest city?

Nor is a mile of salt water, we add, an obstacle between friends. As Jeanne says, "The channel brings out the real ones." One blustery night we were startled by a knock on the door. Lloyd and Ella LaSalle had rowed over, and stood there in dripping rain togs. Lloyd smiled. "Thought you folks would like a game of bridge." An island we believe is only as isolated as you make it.

To be bored is not to enjoy what you are doing. We don't mind hard work, we tell them, if we can see the result of our labor—can shape a plan into a reality, utilize what we build, even plant things and watch them grow. In today's world, few people have the chance. An island is a do-it-yourself life. It's fun as well as a challenge to provide our own shelter, food, fuel, light, and water. To be our own school, our own teachers. In laying a pipeline or shingling a roof, we learn as much (if not more) about ourselves as about water systems or buildings.

Besides, we ask, how can we be bored with so much to do at so little expense? Take a bag of cement, for example, What wonders we can create with our own sand and gravel —landings, walks, walls, and patios, even steps to a porch, or a floor in the roothouse. And what treasures the sea yields for the beachcombing. A chain from a boomstick holds our floats together; a gnarled hunk of drift becomes a lamp to read by. Fir saplings can be cut, peeled, and made into porch rails, fences, or furniture. The cost? Only a little time, enthusiasm, and a bag of nails.

What's more, we tell them, it's exciting to live on a wild wisp of land where nine months of the year there is no human life but our own. It's exhilarating to feel that wherever my foot falls, there may have been no other. Unlike the eight-to-five routine, island life offers a climate of variety. No two jobs, or two days, are alike. Nature is a ceaseless spectacle. An eagle plucking a salmon from the sea is a two-way feast. So is the cormorant's sunset vigil on a sea-washed rock. Nothing is static. The sky, sea, and trees are in constant flux. Even birds, mink, and deer alter their apparel. To live with so much beauty binds one with love—not to a house or its lot, but to the earth itself. For beauty is a great active force; it enlarges thought, promotes sincerity, and deepens feeling. It keeps the heart open, the mind alert. It charges the batteries of wonder and enthusiasm, awakening within us the deep springs which feed the joy of life.

IT'S AUGUST and as hot as ever. Mrs. Raleigh has been here three days. She approached me this morning, before anyone else, rather secretively. "Mr. Conover, is it all right to flush the toilet now?"

Yachtsmen we adore:

The characters who announce their arrival on a loud speaker as if they were the Duke and Duchess of Windsor. Then, as they depart, bellow out, "Good-bye, folks. We're leaving now. See you again soon." (I mutter, "We hope not!")

The blue-denimed brute who struts up to the door, pays his moorage as if it hurts, and exclaims, "Well, what else do we get for our buck and a half?"

The guy who drops anchor for the night, rows his poodle ashore, and returns to his boat without so much as a look or a wave.

The fellow who departs at the crack of dawn, gunning his motors for an eternity as though—at this hour—they needed special prodding.

THESE LAST FEW DAYS I have been working feverishly on the salt water toilet system. Our fresh water will not last. At the same time, I've been hauling over guests and supplies, tending store, checking the well twice daily, servicing motorboats, mowing grass, searching for lost horseshoes, packing wood, cleaning chimney screens, and trying to be pleasant, clean, and cheerful when I feel rude, filthy, and depressed. Today I found it hard to answer Mrs. Raleigh, who asked with rapt seriousness, "Whatever possessed you to buy an island, Mr. Conover?"

After supper the last toilet was hooked up. "You'd better show me how this system works," Jeanne said. "What would happen if you broke a leg or get the mumps from the Martin boy?"

I showed her the floating intake, the pumphouse hidden in the thicket, the switch covered by a piece of tin under the living room window, and then the three-thousand-gallon tank, formerly the kids' plastic swimming pool, which for gravity feed I had located on the hill. We followed the plastic pipe as it snaked through the woods to Crowsnest Cottage. On the outside bathroom wall were two brass valves.

"One is fresh," I explained. "The other—the red one— is salt. It's the same set-up on the rest. Just remember to turn one off before you turn the other on."

Jeanne looked puzzled. "And if I don't?"

"We're out of business." I pointed to the fresh water tank barely visible among the firs. "It's higher than the pool. We have three feet left—less than three thousand gallons. By morning there wouldn't be a drop."

PETER, THE LAD who helped us last summer, is visiting us. He's been in Vancouver, attending the University of British Columbia. When he arrived we were not greeted by "our" Peter, but by his newly acquired "town" personality. "Horrors!" Jeanne remarked when we were alone. "What's happened to Pete? He's gotten so sophisticated I could spank him." In three days we were glad to see the city rubbed off by the abrasiveness of island living.

Nature abhors pretense. She is pledged to naturalness. We are, it seems, the only creatures who refuse to be what we are.

*

Why is it that Americans are afraid to express emotion? When I cut the fish hook from Albert's hand, he didn't even groan! We are ashamed to show feeling. It is thought effeminate, unmanly, and childlike. It is fashionable to live and think without "abandonment." To efface ourselves rather than to give offense; to be insincere rather than not to be likeable; to keep our "cool" rather than show concern. This extraordinary worship of mutual self-respect and pleasantry, like our national paranoia for cleanliness, computerizes the human spirit. When a button is pushed, out come the right words—or the right breath, the right attitude, or the right hairdo. Like the eagle, his national emblem, the American is resourceful, powerful, and proud. But brave—*no!* A single crow, a pair of hummingbirds, puts him to flight. As Wendell Phillips once said, "We are a mass of cowards. More than all other people, we are afraid of each other." Why else do we continually hide behind a smile?

HEAVY LOAD of garbage today. What tales it tells! Mrs. Raleigh is on a diet: the Metracal cans. The two aspirin tins explain Mr. Todd's withdrawn and glum behavior. Spaghetti boxes and sardine tins reveal that the Arnolds are not as wealthy as they'd like us to believe. And the tranquilizers haven't done a thing for the Trotters. But girlie magazines—I didn't expect that of Mr. Snow!

Jeanne shines steadily, under any circumstance—not intermittently as I do. With dull people, my soul flees to a wooden glen and dwells there contentedly until I come for it.

Dickson is a big ruddy American in his fifties with thin red hair, but his face is unlined and boyish. His eyes are deep blue and restless, with a slight hint of melancholy. He has beaten everyone at table tennis. He is a keen fisherman, takes inexhaustible delight in winning at bridge, and completes thirty-two push-ups every morning. He is jovial, wears Hawaiian sport shirts, and speaks with the assurance of a self-made man. This evening he spotted me leveling the horse-shoe pits.

"Don't see how you did it, Dave." His eyes swept the yard and buildings in awe. "A whole island to yourself. How marvelous! This is real living." I smiled faintly. We had been up half the night preparing for new arrivals—scrubbing floors, stoves, and dishes.

"I've spent so much time acquiring things," he went on, "I've never slowed down long enough to enjoy them. I've got a beautiful home on the Russian River with several acres, a yacht I never use. Real estate scattered all over California I've never seen. Three TV sets in the house I'm never home long enough to watch. I have three cars, a half dozen apart-ments, a business in a dozen cities capable of running itself. Yet I run myself ragged trying to visit the branches regularly. What has it all got me? Ulcers, a nagging wife, and children that don't know me. It isn't worth it, Dave. You've got the right idea. Yes, you've got something here."

GOAT'S RUE IS an amazing plant. On Wednesday I shoved a clump in the ground; today it's blooming. Goat's rue never does less than its best. It has the vigor of a dandelion, the beauty and fragrance of sweet peas. Cut it down, it springs up more luxuriant. A perennial that shines in any soil, in any position, and neither insects nor drought affects its exu-berant growth. Would I could meet such a man!

SOMETIMES IT'S a dull, maddening business, this dealing with the public. People always expect more than we are able to give. Mr. Todd was furious when he discovered there was no TV; Mrs. Raleigh, when there was no maid service. Then, in the store today, Mrs. Arnold exclaimed, "No powdered breadcrumbs?" as if she would starve without them.

Fortunately, the island is a great soother of petty cares and frustrations. Nature makes people more human. We become more natural and kind in the wilds. There is a deep desire in everyone for naturalness. Do we not love those best who enjoy us for what we are?

The resort, I confess, has done a lot for me. It has renewed my faith in mankind, which had been sadly shaken by the war. It renewed my interest in human nature, my fascination with what makes people tick. It is intensely satisfying to help someone forget his frets and cares, to see freeway lines vanish from his face, to watch a father get to know his children, to have someone who barely knows you share with you his hopes and dreams. In each person there is something beautiful, and it is with this that we should swear eternal friendship. It makes me, I know, a poor fishing guide. For I find it infinitely more rewarding to explore a human heart than to catch a salmon.

A QUIET SPELL. This August afternoon I climbed the ridge above the cove, sat beneath a coppery madrona, and began to read. In an instant, I was whisked to nineteenth-century London—listening to Hazlitt lecture, admiring the Elgin marbles at the British Museum, and—as a medical student—going from ward to ward in Guys Hospital dressing surgical wounds. It was later than I thought when I returned to the house.

Jeanne looked alarmed. "Where have you been?"

"With Keats," I replied.

A Seattle man forgot his keys. Poor fellow! He was nearly frantic until we found and returned them. How fortunate we are. What we value most can't be lost or carted away.

I HAVE DEVELOPED an aversion to Saul Richards. A sort of fancy Dan, he wears alligator shoes, white shirt, and tie when he fishes. Reminds me of a car salesman turned politician —smug and officious. A member of an un-American affairs committee. This afternoon I caught him pulling out library books and stacking them on the Ping-Pong table.

"That's quite a bit of reading," I said with forced humor. "Think you can get through all those?"

"No," he retorted. "Those shouldn't *be* in the library. They're subversive propaganda."

My eyes caught some of the titles: *Death of a Salesman, The Enduring Mind.* I felt my face tighten. "How come you overlooked Plato's *Republic?* Isn't it rather subversive?"

"That's different." He pointed. "These books are written by known members of the Party. . . ." Not caring to prolong the disagreement, I returned the books to the shelves and retreated to the store.

IN BED ONE NIGHT, Jeanne said, "I'm worried. Davey has been acting so strange lately. He seems to disappear for the longest spells. Have you noticed?"

"No," I replied. "Just that he's been hanging around guests a lot. Nothing to worry about. I'm sure he isn't a nuisance. It'll do him good to mix with people."

"Hope you're right, Dave." And we dozed off.

On Wednesday, it was after dark when I got back with the fishing party. Jeanne met me at the door. She looked upset, but she smiled, "Davey isn't asleep yet. I think he's waiting for you."

I went into the bedroom.

"How many did you get, Papa? Any big ones?"

"Five—one twenty-six-pounder."

"Was he a fighter?"

"Yup. He took out five hundred feet of line. Really made it sing. Had to chase him in the boat, but we got him." I tucked the covers around his shoulders. "It's almost eleven. You get some sleep, Big Boy. I'll show him to you in the morning."

Later, sitting at the table over tea, I glanced at Jeanne. She is especially pretty when she is disturbed. "All right, out with it, Angel. What's wrong?"

"Davey." She put her cup down. "I didn't want to say anything till he was asleep. You know his, *big* ears." And she paused.

"Well?"

"I found this hidden in the closet." She emptied the contents from a toffee tin into her hand—$2.50 in coins. "Where do you suppose he got it?"

I was startled. "From the store?"

"No, thank goodness. The cash drawer checks out okay."

"Where, then?" We both knew guests left their cottages unlocked and were outside most of the day.

She bit her lip. "I don't know . . . don't like to think . . . We'll ask him in the morning."

The lights suddenly grew brighter. One of our cottagers had gone to bed. I looked at the voltmeter that sat above the stove.

"Voltage is high enough to do a wash," I said. "Do you feel like it?" We often did the laundry at night. It saved running the generator during the day.

We were tired and depressed, but Jeanne nodded. "We'd better. There's a pile of dirty clothes, and we're almost out of sheets."

I brought the laundry bags over and we began putting the clothes in the tub. A slip of paper from Davey's pants fell on the floor.

"There's something on it," said Jeanne.

In large, wobbly letters, it read: "TOORS. . . . 50 sents
—to the deers, eagel nests, minks houses and Chinees fort.
See me, Davey."

As our eyes met, we burst into laughter.

MRS. JEWETT: A tall, coldly beautiful woman with fine Nordic
features and a self-conscious air. Perhaps thirty, she is ac-
customed to money and moves with the slow deliberateness
of an animated mannequin. Her hips are boyish, but her
breasts are full, delightfully pear-shaped and borne with im-
mense satisfaction. Her low-cut blouses reveal a cleavage that
hinders every shuffleboard game. She reminds Jeanne of
someone she had seen modeling mink in *Vogue*. My impression is that she might have been a nightclub entertainer. The
four children are like her—snobbish, aggressive, and atrociously spoiled.

We knew she had come to the wrong resort the moment
we saw her. Much older, Jewett is a quiet, amiable little man,
very shy, with soft blue eyes and rather pathetic look. He
loves fishing, and does nothing else. How he talked her into
coming, we're eager to find out!

In reply to Will's letter:

> *Glad that I was able to lure you out of the shadows.*
> *I like fire in a man, even if I get scorched. However, I*
> *regret that my hypothetical question (re. money) back-*
> *fired. Just sloppy writing. I know well how you feel on*
> *the subject. I can only go partway. As I see it, the value*
> *of money is in making enough to become independent*
> *of it. For it isn't the money we* have *that makes us a*
> *slave, but the money we hope to make.*
>
> *On both scores—we're safe. We have no fears of*
> *falling into the income tax bracket.*

As to material things, I value them only if they leave me freer for creative work and worthy pursuits. Living with beauty makes one live for beauty—whether it's in a boat, a book, or a man. Nature makes one immune to luxury. In her presence, as Camus said of his mother, "I feel that I belong to a noble race—one that envies nothing."

Now let's talk about W. D. I admire you, Will. Your strength of character, the way you can manage life. Your steadfastness, loyalty to your beliefs, integrity, and honesty. You are an unusual man. You are also well-rounded—a broadcaster, journalist, sailor, teacher, and a damn good writer. What raises my hackles is— why don't you get busy on your real work? I remember, years ago you played us a tape revealing your innermost thoughts. Great stuff! Real stuff—the real Will Dawson. What keeps you from working them into a book?

I'M STILL RAGING. "Positively NO TRESPASSING" doesn't mean a thing anymore. This afternoon I caught campers with their boat pulled up on the beach and gear spread out, building a fire in front of the sign. I was so thunderstruck, I just stood and stared at them. Looking a little ashamed, they collected their things and departed without a word.

"I'd have told those people a thing or two," Jeanne said when I reported the incident. "You shouldn't have let them off so easily."

We spent all evening raking the yard. Cursed madrona leaves! It's a ceaseless, endless downpour. Wherever there is a madrona, it's always fall. And if we're not raking, we're mowing, pruning, or whacking.

"Sometimes it worries me, Dave." Jeanne's eyes were suddenly grave. "We aren't getting any younger. What happens when we won't be able to keep up the place?"

I considered that. "You know the point on Princess Harbor. Well, I see a beautiful house, flowering shrubs, an oystershell lawn, a gangway right into the kitchen."

"You dreamer." She grinned.

I HAVE BEEN thinking about what happened the other day. Not that people do not respect private property or read signs anymore, but wondering whether my reaction was correct. Jeanne has made it clear you've got to be tough with your rights or people will walk all over you. To me, this is not the issue. Why should I let people dictate—even when they step on my toes—the way I should act? Because they have no manners is no reason why I should lose mine.

THE LAST WEEK has been hectic. Mrs. Jewett has given her kids paring knives to open oysters, which is like opening a vault with a screwdriver. We've run out of patience. So has Wallie, who has been the target for their spears. Battered pots and pans litter the beach, horseshoes have been flung into the bush, and path-gravel strewn on the lawn. At noon there was a loud crash. Jeanne rushed into the store. "The luggage cart," she cried. "The little monsters have smashed it into a tree."

But nothing seems to bother Mrs. Jewett. Not even the bill. All morning she fusses and primps, trying on clothes or fashioning hairdos to wear in the afternoon. Today she emerged from the cottage at four like a duchess bound for a ball. We chuckled. Everyone had gone fishing.

We have had to revise our opinion of yachtsmen. A burly, baldheaded chap in tan bermudas came ashore tonight, paid his moorage, and after looking around, rested his hand on his grandson's shoulder. He said, "Don't you wish our San Juan place was as lovely as this?"

Later, someone asked, "Did you know who that was?"

I shook my head.

"Henry J. Kaiser."

AT BREAKFAST, Jeanne suggested: "Let's have a lamb barbecue. The guests will love it."

I cast a serious eye at her.

"It won't be any trouble. Really," she added.

I visioned otherwise. "Who's going to shoot the bugger, gut and dress him, collect wood for the fire, spend hours in the sun rotating and basting the beast, then clean up all the mess and litter?"

"I'll help," Davey chimed. "I know where the sheeps are. Shall I get the gun?" The sheep were quite wild, even wilder than the deer.

"All right," I gave in reluctantly. "I suppose an orgy now and then won't hurt."

The little band of sheep and several lambs were grazing in the meadow. "We must make sure to get a boy lamb," I said to Davey as we crept up. "Best to save the females for breeding."

"How can you tell?" He stared at them. "They look alike."

Never having been sheared, they were indeed hard to distinguish. "We'll just have to trust to luck," I replied, raising the rifle, "and hope we get a male. (I felt rather smug about my cleverness in avoiding a genital analysis of the sexes.)

The first shot missed. The second bagged a male—pure luck—as they charged into the bush. While I gutted the animal, Davey brought up the luggage cart; then we packed the carcass to the beach near the house. I began to build a fire.

"Not wood!" Jeanne exclaimed over the fence. "Use bark. It doesn't give as much smoke and ash." She eyed the lamb. "Gee, I thought it would be larger than that. You'd better dig some clams. Get some oysters too. Oh yes, we'll need more butter, and we're nearly out of pop." A sudden chill of panic swept my spine.

Lamb Barbecue on the Beach

By the time the lamb was stretched on the spit over the coals, we had a gathering of supervisors: The fire was too hot. No—the rotation was too fast (some said not fast enough). After sampling the basting, Mrs. Horowitz cried, "For God's sake, did you forget the salt?" Kids stuck their dirty fingers into the meat. Poked the carcass with sticks. One poked too hard. The lamb fell into the coals. We scraped off the ashes (I could have mangled that boy!) and washed down the remainder with the hose.

As hours slipped by—between sun and fire—shouts came from the bank like a volley of gunshots. Have you sharpened the carving knife? Are there ice cubes in the fridge? Did you find the egg slicer? Salad isn't large enough—better hop over and get a couple of heads from Myrt. . . . What about seats? Bring up every available plank—all the chairs. . . . Oh yes, ask Myrt if she has any paper plates. . . . Tell everyone to bring their silver and cups. No, better not—just the cups. Well, don't stand there—do something!"

So went the day.

Toward eight, guests sauntered onto the beach, freshly bathed and immaculately dressed in sporty attire. We staggered from the fire to greet them, groggy from smoke, sun, and confusion, with hands splotched with Band-Aids covering second-degree burns. All evening, as I sat on the log and exchanged pleasantries, I thought how simple it all would have been with hamburgers.

DAVEY HAS quite a system. He catches a shiner at the wharf, puts it on a hook, and pulls in a cod; lowers the cod head in the crab pot, then uses the largest crab to bait the box trap in order to catch a live mink—which, in turn, he shows to people for two bits a "look"!

9:20 A.M. Distress call from Crowsnest.
9:30 A.M. Brought plumbing snake to the scene.

9:50 A.M. Managed to relieve congestion.

There are two occasions when we can *always* expect interruption: sitting at a meal or on the toilet. Life here keeps us erect.

THE CART GROANED. At last we were pushing Mrs. Jewett's pyramid of luggage toward the wharf. "You know I'd rather stay here," Jewett said wistfully. "I hate plush resorts and crowds. But I promised Clare if we could come here, I'd take her to Banff. I'm not sorry that I did."

We, however, were not sorry to see them go.

Nature is a great democrat. This afternoon Jeanne spotted a rowboat off the point and reached for the binoculars. "It's Gardner and Mulloy," she gasped. "Our butcher boy fishing with the bank president. What Levi's and a fishing line won't do!"

FOR SEVERAL DAYS now the rain has confined guests to their cottages, and the air has the damp smell of evergreens and smoke. In the store, there's been a run on cocoa, marshmallows, popping corn, and postcards. The drizzle doesn't seem to bother anyone except the Hoveys—a Santa Barbara couple. They have contracted a bad case of disillusionment. The first symptom appeared Wednesday when he sputtered, "Does it always rain here, Mr. Conover?" A Californian, it seems, knows only two catastrophes: the earthquake and the rain cloud.

While unpacking stock behind the store I heard a familiar voice. "It's stopped raining, Mommy. Can we go on a picnic?"

"No, not today."

"Why?"

"Your father and I are busy—can't you see? Besides, who would watch the store?"

"To Pebble Beach . . . with pop and potato chips, huh, Mom?"

"No."

"Front of the house, where the mink lives?"

A slight pause. "We'll see. . . . Maybe."

At noon, I put the note on the door: "Back in an hour, maybe."

On the rocks, we spread out our lunch. The cove was agleam in the silvery sunlight; the yachts at the wharf shone like white jewels, and people were scrubbing decks, laughing, and drinking beer. We had no sooner finished the peanut butter sandwiches than a sloop rounded the point and came in the gap.

"It's the Stokleys," Jeanne exclaimed as the boat dropped its sails. "I bet they're after another baby."

Their batting average is 100 percent here—nine months after each visit! He's a fragile man in his fifties, but Irma's still in her twenties—shapely and pretty as a Pepsi-Cola ad, and speaks with charming naïveté.

"It's the water," she confided to Jeanne, after her last baby was born. "When we were here last we drank gallons. It makes Harold virile, I believe." We had to admit there was something to it. Harold was transferred to Hawaii, where they lived for two years. Not until they returned to Wallace did she become pregnant again.

We greeted them at the wharf. Harold had aged considerably; his scanty hair was white now, and he had the look of a weathered oak, as the three children tugged at him. "We're back again, Dave." He nodded toward Irma. "Nothing'll stop her until the works give out!"

We have no reliable evidence to prove 'it's the water.

It's our hunch that it has to do more with the island than anything else. The great outdoors not only extends life, but adds to our species as well.

IN THE WOODBIN this morning, we heard a faint chirping. "Crickets!" Jeanne said. "Seems like summer just began."

Fall

I challenge anyone to stand with Autumn on a hilltop and fail to see a new expanse not only around him, but in him, too.

—Hal Borland

JEANNE AND DAVEY ENJOY THE AUTUMN WOODS

DAY AFTER LABOR DAY. How quiet! We feel like an occupied territory abandoned by a conquering army. The lawn chairs are empty, the boats lie idle, the wharf is bare of yachtsmen. It is so still we can hear the pigeons devour the madrona berries. Davey is lost without playmates, and Wallie wanders hopefully from cottage to cottage looking for handouts.

"We should be happy," Jeanne said. "We've got the island to ourselves again."

But we aren't—not yet anyway.

AUTUMN ARRIVES at some unappointed time, like the tax assessor.

We don't have to see September to know it's here. We hear it in the crickets' chorus, the symphony of humming insects, the tumble of falling leaves. We can feel it in the dryness of the nostrils, the parchedness of the forest on the lips; smell it in the spicy fragrance of summer-weary cedars. The maples have turned to gold, and near the workshop, the chokecherry's green umbrella is now a stark skeleton against

89

the autumn sky. Nature has begun to unwind and relax after the travail of summer. It's time for us to refresh and rebuild, too.

A moonlight picnic on the beach tonight. The firelight didn't warn us when the tide—before we knew it—crept in and soaked our feet. As it doused the fire it became a catastrophe. "Now we've got to eat *raw* marshmallows," Davey groaned.

IT'S BEEN A WEEK since the exodus. The aloneness seems strange, the silence disturbing. We keep hearing voices, the laughter of children, the hum of cruisers, and the clatter of shuffleboard. We keep chuckling over Mrs. Tooley—the matronly Azusa schoolteacher who, while tracking a kingfisher with her binoculars, lost her footing and splashed into the cove. We remember the delightful Krueger family—the five sleuths who unearthed primitive artifacts on Panther Point, and we can still see Henry Grandon in his baggy pants and jaunty cap, wandering down the path to his boat.

DAVE WEATHERALL dropped by today. I am amazed at the quiet strength and knowledgeable ways of these commercial fishermen. While he picked a bucket of plums, I picked his mind. An hour never went by so swiftly. What nuggets I found—about squirrels, motors, Mexico, and TV reception (nary a word about fish). I am sure I got the best of the exchange.

In the city one wonders how to dispose of one's time; in the country, one wonders how to dispose of his tin cans.

Sometimes I think that we kill our pets with kindness. How pudgy Wallie has become! He trails behind on our walks —no spark, no gaiety. "We'd better cut his food," I said, reaching into the cookie jar. "It'll increase his life and vigor."

"Not a bad idea"—Jeanne eyed my waistline—"for you either."

SINCE MONDAY we've been bedding down the cottages, draining the plumbing, and storing the linen. I put antifreeze in the traps, capped the chimneys, and cleaned the fireplaces. Boats, the garden, other fall chores, can wait, for I am growing impatient to start on the book again. I am an old bear who wants into his den.

What a surprise! Dr. Mac rowed over this evening. He'll be eighty-four tomorrow. Quite an accomplishment even for a young man. Yet who, besides Vic, *rows* these days, in this age of outboards? He's looked upon as either foolish or overly frugal. Dr. Mac, of course, is neither. What better way to keep younger than your years.

We welcomed him at the wharf. "Rowed too fast, I guess," he said, nodding at the pole. "The fish couldn't keep up with me."

Dr. Mac is a serene man, tall and dignified as a stately fir. His eyes are deep set and wise, and gentleness radiates from his face, which is etched by a thousand smiles. He handed Jeanne the bouquet of flowers.

"Homegrown and handpicked"—he grinned boyishly— "for the first lady of Wallace."

Like so many vintage islanders, Dr. Mac is timeless. No one would suspect his age. He's into everything—chairman of hospital and library boards, Wall Street speculator, gardener unrivaled, party goer and giver, and forever alert to worthy causes, giving both his time and money. Age is something other people worry about. I had to know the secret of his perpetual youth.

"Get involved," he said simply. "Get into things that will be around long after you've gone."

*

Ducks are returning from their vacations. A few fat mallards flew in today and raised quite a ruckus among the permanent dwellers. "You'd think," Jeanne remarked, "the kingfishers owned the place, by the fuss they make."

A LETTER this afternoon from Will declares he cannot write what he really wants to until he feels ready. The time is not yet ripe. Oh, my dear Will—the right moment *never* comes. Imperfection is the rule of life. We must constantly overlook what we are, to do the great thing. Achievement depends more on courage than talent dares admit.

He also says, "Real thoughts will out," which sounds vaguely as if he depends on inspiration. Thoreau declared, "A man has no suspicion of his thoughts until his pen discovers them." Perspiration is the thing. Persistence. Get into the material. Grub. Momentum will come. Everyone is an oracle of the human condition. People do want to hear what a writer wishes to say—for every sincere thought born of a personal conviction is of interest or use to someone.

What an absurd thing, said Gide, this fear of the self in literature; this fear of talking of oneself, of being interested in oneself, of showing oneself. If now and again the superior person does not confide to us of himself, there would be no great books.

It wasn't until I came to the island that I realized one does not become a man until he learns to be alone.

Solitude is the air I love to breathe. The days I don't see anyone are the most pleasurable to me. When I am with people, I lose something of myself. However, my solitude does not belong to me—when I am alone I see how much it belongs to others.

THE FIRST RAIN in a long while—a good excuse to write and avoid chores.

As a writer I am destined to be a short-order cook. I can dish up only small books. For I have neither the capacity for nor the knack of preparing sumptuous dinners. I must resign myself to assembling sentences, where most writers assemble pages; must obtain satisfaction from turning out an essay, where others achieve classic tomes. I am like Joubert—"Words take their revenge on me by their difficulty." Perhaps it's just as well. My passion—like his—is to bull's-eye the truth, not to build a house with it. To treat it gently and briefly, with joy, so it may illuminate the hearts of men.

WE PICKED BARTLETTS this afternoon and packed them in the root cellar. One weighed over a pound. Why are the largest always at the top? Times like these I'm all for progress. What a godsend an aluminum ladder is! Our generating plant, too, and gas refrigerator. Could we go back to gas lamps and cooler? A woman—rarely. But the simple life is one of man's most persistent dreams. Inside every business suit is a Crusoe who cries to be set free.

Nature welcomes us as royalty. How pleasant the trails are, cushioned by the broadloom of fallen leaves. Yet I cannot bear to step on a fir cone, for it holds so much promise.

MORE LOCAL VISITORS. We appreciate their thoughtfulness in waiting till after the summer rush. Besides, we're selfish. We want our friends all to ourselves.

ON LOOKING BACK at this year's crop of guests, I find it disturbing that I can remember only a few. The majority leave no impression, no peculiarity that lingers, and fade quickly from memory. So many witless grins, limpid handshakes, pleasing overtures; so few faces that reflect clear-cut character. Sincerity, I fear, has succumbed to agreeableness. We are too well disposed toward too much. It's a trait that muddies the function of the best-defined man. A solvent that levels down the human flesh.

What *is* average? What is normal, but a statistic of concession? Those who are more like others than unique individuals. I prefer to meet with my opposite, whom I may profit by, who has an abrasiveness to sharpen my outlook, an unexpected quirk of character that will whet my curiosity: "Some provoking strangeness," said Thoreau, "so that we may be guest and host and refresh one another." A man possesses significance only by virtue of being considerably abnormal. The so-called normal person is usually so deadly dull that I cherish every eccentric I meet.

Scientists are keen on determining if Mars has an atmosphere. I am more concerned that a man has one—what Virginia Woolf calls "something central that permeates."

THIS MORNING Davey strolled by the window, fishing rod in hand, toward the wharf. I was busy writing, desperately trying to stick to my routine. Then it struck me. Why should the morning be sacred? I grabbed the pole behind the door and hurried down the path. We hopped in the rowboat. The sea was gunmetal calm, the air milky with shrouds of pearly mist. I felt better behind the oars, looking into Davey's shining face. His reward was generous. "Glad you came along, Papa."

IF IT IS POSSIBLE to love and hate the same thing, the madrona is the culprit. Of all trees, it is the most maddening—and the most beautiful. It is strikingly feminine, brash and sensu-

DAVEY FISHING FROM THE WHARF

ous, flouting its coppery nakedness amidst the blush of stately firs and cedars.

By nature and by habit, the madrona is female. Though an evergreen, she is always changing her mind, disrobing like a harlot for every season. Her trunk and limbs are a bright cinnamon in summer, a sunburnt orange in fall. As the days grow colder, the madrona greets winter in olive green, which

A PEELING MADRONA

she suddenly discards for a tan frock with the first warm rays of the sun.

Typically female, the madrona is rarely silent. The slightest breeze is like a tidbit of gossip, exciting a flurry of chatter amongst her leaves. On wintry days, her delicate limbs groan and snap like gunshots in the frosty air. In summer, you hear her peel and crackle as her bark curls into bits of parchment and tumbles to the forest floor.

With feminine tenacity, she thrives where other trees refuse to grow—on rocky ledges, arid windswept promontories. She blossoms the most profusely in the poorest soil. Death is never sudden. Her sinewy limbs wither, one by one, waxing a silvery gray like gnarled and majestic arms of supplication.

The madrona is a joy all winter. Her festive red berries are a splash of color among the somber evergreens. And after a rain, her foliage shines like chartreuse umbrellas held up by copper canes. But—oh, my! In summer, the madrona is the meanest, dirtiest thing alive. There is seldom a moment she isn't shedding—either leaves, bark, berries, or flowers. Berries stain concrete, leaves are the devil to rake. Slippery and brittle, they break into bits, clog the rake, and fray the nerves, trailing a sea of brown confetti across the grass. How does one cope with such an ornery creature? "I'll tell you," Jeanne cries when her blisters smart. "Get me the ax!" Oddly enough, I can never remember where I put it.

MET MRS. TAYLOR at Fernwood today coming back from Swenson's. What distressing modesty: her poems show great promise, but she hasn't the heart to submit them for publication. Had it not been for her friend, Mrs. Ritchie, I never would have known. . . . I must do something!

Each person brings something precious into the world that has never before existed. It is a marvelous process in the devious ways it unfolds. While overseas in the Air Force, I had a buddy named Smitty. In civilian life he was a gas station operator. On Leyte he ran the officers' mess, a job he fell into entirely by accident. When I was not out on assignment, I ate with him in the dining room (a very salutary thing for a private). The food was superb, and one look around told me he knew instinctively how to run a kitchen. Also, the way he decorated the tables and the bar and served food left no doubt that he was a natural restaurateur.

"Smitty, why don't you start on your own when you get out?"

He chuckled. "Running a mess is not like running a supper club."

"Way you do it, it is," I replied. "Now who would ever think of sticking a sign on a baked potato—'I'm scrubbed, you can eat *all* of me'?"

My constant needling must have sunk in. After the war, Smitty turned his gas station into a drive-in and kept enlarging it until a few years later it became Oxnard's famous Colonial Inn.

I have been rereading my journals. How sententious they are! A hunter with a skyful of geese who must make a dozen shots to wing one truth.

WE'RE AT LOW EBB. Jeanne has just finished the accounts. We made—after expenses—$851.50 this season. She wonders if running the resort is worth it. "That's not much for all our hard work." Her eyes were tense with worry. "Barely enough to scrape by."

"You know, don't you"—she became very grave—"one poor season will wipe us out?"

I tried to cheer her. "Angel, all we need is more cottages. The next one we build will be pure gravy. After all, there's a gamble to anything worthwhile." I pointed to the book I was writing.

"What if it doesn't sell?"

Her words came as a shock. I was too busy writing to consider that possibility.

That's the basic difference between man and woman. A

man's life is his work; a woman's work (should be), a man's life. As a woman owes herself to one, a man owes himself to all. His are long goals, hers are short-term. She wants *results*. A man can wait—he lives by challenge and struggle. A woman prefers a cloudless, more comfortable present. She won't gamble on a hazy future; a man invariably will.

When we bought the island we didn't realize the bargain we had in mink, eagles, and deer; neither did we know that we were buying a monstrous "status symbol." Abroad, every American is considered wealthy, but add the opulence of island ownership and you've become a multimillionaire. Island poor—what a paradox! How fortunate we are to be blessed with so rich a poverty.

I SOMETIMES THINK a person writes best anonymously. How bold, pure, and sweet do we speak from our private heart. No wonder Gide exclaimed, "Ah, the happy time when I was not listened to!" What author has not faltered because of fame? Who manages "to keep his life in hand," as Hal Borland asks, "and go on writing worthy books?" An audience is like a dog that turns on its master. It seeks to maim or destroy what it loves. For a man is easier robbed of his potential than of his wealth. Creation requires character as much as talent. It requires constraint—a ruthless sincerity. To be constant to oneself involves a sort of deafness to others. I wonder, can I be spotlighted and remain whole?

A man is admirably equipped to withstand any circumstance, any travail but success. I have an abnormal fear of it. Down deep, I feel weak to the world's pull . . . apprehensive that it will disturb or impair my way of living. For my life and art are one. Creativity is the child of solitude. When Thoreau hied himself to Walden, it was not to study nature but to learn more about himself. Wallace is my pond.

My first saga is only an apprenticeship. My real work

lies ahead, ripening like a pear in my root cellar. I have no hankering to be a popular writer. If I appeal, it will be to the thoughtful few. I'd rather touch than shine, rather irritate than entertain. The triumph of a writer is to disturb a person's destiny. To make him think. Men ply the sea of life with rarely enough sail, barely enough ballast, content to reside in the fo'c'sle of least exertion. I would hail them on deck, proclaim them divine creatures, remind them they are not pawns of fate but gods of their own creation. What is more tragic than to discover, in the rubble of the past, the person we might have been?

IT'S NEARLY OCTOBER NOW. This morning a seaplane flew over with a horrendous screech and shortly afterward, as I looked from the window, a great blue heron rose noisily in the air.

Thumbnail of Max: about thirty-five, married; neat, scrubbed look. On the short, stocky side. Deep voice. Sensitive lips and dark, honest eyes.

Questions everything: not satisfied with simple explanations.

German stubbornness, thoroughness, exactness.

Proud of his frugality: "I have no qualms. A boat means fish in the freezer or bark in the shed—nothing else."

A grease pit in the garage doubles as a root cellar.

Buys things to save money: wood furnace, so that he can use drift logs for fuel—Mildred complains of the cold mornings.

Master electrician; efficient and quick. Works only when he feels like it. Mildred doesn't permit him to discuss religion with customers—he loses too many.

Hates worse: traveling sixteen miles to fix a light switch.

Loves best: his "ham" shack, where he retreats from the world in order to converse with it.

Reads good books, finishing high school by correspondence.

Shy mannerisms: "Now let me see." He fingers an earlobe.

I like Max. He has an innate sense of finding good that one would expect of a more educated man. *Not* a backwoods tradesman.

WE SAT FOR a long while at the cove's edge, listening to Tchaikovsky's Fifth Symphony pouring from the speaker on the rocks.

"It's like the Hollywood Bowl," Jeanne whispers.

"With kingfishers and mink for an audience," I added. Several jaunty fellows—those steady divers—sat motionless on madrona limbs while on an outcrop of sandstone our gourmet squatted with beady-eyed serenity.

Music and nature are natural partners. They are a cathartic that purges us of the poisons of daily living. The calm by which we repossess our souls. They invite us to rise above our everyday selves, to partake of our legacy and live more fully.

Music, to me, is as essential as the air I breathe. On grizzly days, the longing becomes almost a physical thirst. A Chopin Nocturne brightens the atmosphere as it nourishes the soul. In Debussy's ethereal realm I consort with my loftiest thoughts, dream that I am brave enough to live them. Like nature, music brings into harmony all that is beautiful within, brings out all the best we are.

What a grand symphony the heart and intellect make of a common inspiration, conducted by truth!

On our walks, at bedtime, the moon spreads a fine snow among the firs.

*

I never feel more alive than when I go after the mail on a blustery day. The channel is sweet to overcome. I return a conqueror—if only with a mail-order circular!

Those who know something of the prose and poetry of mankind will recognize that though I possess only one tongue, I sometimes have many voices. My peers trip me up. They steal into mind and disguise their thoughts as my own. Of this charlatanry, I am neither ashamed or fearful, as I am a gathering of love—a compendium of worship. I loot with a pirate's skill all the heart will possess, all the spirit will absorb. Possession may signify ownership under civil law, but I am the servant of a higher law, which declares acquisition can be purchased only by love. The State may call me thief; to a higher State of Being, I am a common citizen exercising a natural right.

Life is not democratic. The highest offices of mankind are not open to election, but to a man's own choosing.

Who has not sold out to the engagement book?
How many of us fritter ourselves away, when—if given a monk's cell—we could have come up with something.

ON MONDAY Davey and I set off on a cruise of the islands. We spent the night on Dinner Island, a small green drop in fjord-like Saanich Inlet. The shoreline is sharp blue shale, nearly straight up and down, and it was almost dark before we got our gear ashore and camp laid out. Davey insisted I had anchored on the wrong side. (Wallie was noncommittal.) I insisted the boat was safe. What possible wind could blow straight down from the sky?

After wieners and beans, we crawled into our bags and snuggled before the fire. The hum of traffic on the Malahat Drive, magnified a thousand times by the canyon walls,

DINNER ISLAND

sounded as if we were sprawled under a freeway. As I dozed off, the shrill blast of a freight train bolted me upright. Finally I fell asleep, only to awaken, startled by trees whooshing overhead and leaves pelting my face. Grabbing the flashlight, I struck out for the boat. The anchor had dragged. Luminous waves were on the verge of battering her on the rocks. Quickly, I leapt aboard and anchored on the quiet side.

In the morning, Davey's serious face hovered over me. "I told you so, Papa, but you wouldn't listen."

Now I am mourning my lost divinity. There's nothing like a camping trip to show a father how fallible he is!

I am plagued by the feeling that I am inadequately equipped to write. Perhaps I perceive the terrible responsibility of the printed word—that it can change a life, that the truth I know may not be the universal truth I seek, that I might mislead unknowingly. The *Good Housekeeping* article "We Bought an Island" brought letters that shook me with the bleakness of many lives, all pinning their hopes on island living as the answer. "Escape from" is rarely successful. One must be "drawn toward." I must make this clear.

The poet Winfield Townley Scott wrote: "Words are very powerful. You aren't sure of that? Think of all the things you won't say."

NATURE IS LAZILY closing up shop, dazzling us with her garments of yellows and browns. We are not far behind; the fireplace is repaired, the gutters cleared, and summer togs packed away. The crickets have lost their voices. Bracken sprawls like golden lace beneath the firs, and smoke from burning slashings scents the air. Maples stand naked and motionless, braced for winter gales. Beside the garden, where potatoes are yellowing, petunias and snapdragons nod weary

Davey and Wallie Watch a Freighter Go By

heads. The soft, swift October twilights pulsate with the drowsy hum of insects, the whisper of falling leaves, the faint chirpings of towhees in the bush. Everything has slackened, even my heartbeat. Where once I rushed to the wharf, now I saunter like a billowy cloud across the autumn sky.

I have contracted a severe case of "bookitis"—a rash accompanied by high fever that invariably occurs in the fall. It is rarely fatal, but the symptoms usually last till spring. The only effective drug is print, the side effects of which induce laziness, a pronounced revulsion for work, a state of euphoria, and a decided churlishness in one's mate. Lately I turn down a dozen books for every one I pick up. I am devouring Matthew Arnold in the bathroom, Goethe on the sofa, and Seneca in bed.

THE OTHER EVENING Davey looked thoughtfully at me. "Why do you read so much, Papa?" he asked, climbing into my lap.

"Curious, I guess—want to learn more."

"Why? Didn't you go to school?"

"Yes, but I didn't pay attention."

"Why?"

"I wasn't very smart."

He frowned curiously. "Weren't there any teachers?"

"Uh-huh. Some good ones."

"Why didn't they make you smart?"

I shrugged. "Too deaf, I guess. Everything went in one ear, out the other."

"Didn't you go to a doctor?"

As I look back, I can see Davey was right. My head should have been examined.

What long patience and discipline it costs to overcome the handicaps of one's youth. I was raised by a father I never saw and a mother who was rarely at home. The education

I received at five private schools, like a vaccination, never took, and a war intervened before I became a college dropout. Now the island is my school, books are my teachers. To write is to expose oneself. If I am going to share what I am, I must constantly go on learning and trying to become a better person.

Clifton Fadiman struck a truth when he said: "All true education is a delayed-action bomb, assembled in the classroom for explosion at a later date." It's a pity that so much time is wasted on growing up!

Boyhood holds no special charm that manhood does not surpass in a grander way. In youth I was all senses and limbs, with only rare twitches of intellect. Now I have more youthful instincts than when I was young, and nothing do I find as luxuriant as my thoughts. In fact, it frightens me that I can live so easily off my spiritual stores.

What does the spirit devour?

Books, music, and paintings; sunsets, mountains, and sea; friends, noble thoughts, the excellence of things—and time to contemplate all of these.

ANOTHER INDIAN SUMMER DAY—still, warm, and shining. This afternoon I chopped kindling, picked the last green tomatoes, and mulched the carrots and leeks. Kitchen has a heavenly aroma—Jeanne is busy preserving pears and plums.

Vic picks up Pete, the little lame pug, with the gentle hands with which he touches all living things. What a father he would have made to the boy I was in my youth!

In reading Eckermann's *Conversations with Goethe*, I am like a moth drawn to light. I can't resist worshiping this amazing man. Where most authors are ponds, Goethe is an ocean. I can easily drown myself in him, for he embraces with ease the entire realm of human experience and thought. To walk with him is to find everything interesting—a leaf, a pebble, a gnarled man, or an epoch. Every page reveals the sweep of his great hospitable mind, the calm, mellow touch of his wisdom. I am having a delightful time, but desperately afraid I'll make every word my own. On page 161, however, Goethe has soothed me. "Only by making the riches of others our own do we bring anything great into being." As it takes many streams to make a broad river, so a man's stature is revealed by his tributaries.

MORE GLORIOUS DAYS. They have brought us friends and, from our beachcombing, a fresh supply of bark and timbers for the shed. We've been raking leaves into piles of gold. Davey stomps on them like a wild Indian. "Even if it doesn't blow," Jeanne cried, "the yard will be rid of them!"

Wasps hunger over decayed fallen apples, clumsy and aimless, as if intoxicated by the rancid scent.

How barren one's life would be without the changing seasons. When I remember those years in Los Angeles, where one can tell October only on the calendar, they are marked by an emptiness, as if I had not lived them. I was a digit in the census; all surface and no core. Alas—a fingerprint in search of entity!

Where the days are alike, men are too much alike. Nothing differs in the human landscape but fashion and opinion. And the six o'clock news. Without winter, human nature blurs and repeats itself. We dwell on the surface of our skins. The atmosphere has no weather; no grit or sand to form character. To stretch the soul. For how else, except by the continuous irritation of a grain of sand, does the oyster fashion a pearl? An endless summer is but a profusion of light, which browns the body as it withers the soul. If Concord had lain on the banks of the San Gabriel Wash, would she have produced such illustrious men?

The orb of man is a small globe. The seasons must revolve around him if he is to come into season within. The systolic and diastolic pulsebeat of nature—of day and night, of calm and storm, of youth and age—is much like our own. Our soil is the compost of Octobers. We are June seeded. A promise fall itself redeems.

I love the seasons so well that I am glad nature is fond of repeating them. In winter, I become an island within myself, thrown on my own resources and experiments. I take joyous little excursions into my interior to improve the inland trade of thought and ideas, so I may enhance my commerce in the outer world. As summer delights the body with health and action, winter delights the mind with thoughts and vigor. I beachcomb the bookshelves to relive Hannibal's march across the Alps, enjoy the high adventure of living in great minds, design and build a small-scale floating boathouse for the launch. Summer proves our dexterity, but it's December that proves our grit; in winter we become more nearly what we are.

IN SPEAKING of the desert enemy, T. E. Lawrence said, "One must risk oneself a hundred times, to learn." I wonder if this is not also true of love, and that its greatest enemy is personal cowardice. To learn—to grasp the full knowledge of things—one must risk loving. For one learns only what one has the courage to love.

Davey is ever asking questions, ever wanting to know. He exposes my ignorance with such tenderness that I am sure he thinks, "What a child my father is!"

DEAR GOD, give me the courage to dwell outside myself so that I won't stand in my own way . . . so that I may be free of the poisoning of vanity, envy, and malice . . . that I may not easily judge . . . may not easily make comparisons, but be able to see in each man something greater than his every-day self.

STILL OCTOBER, and the cottages are battened, the boats put away, and the garden mulched for frost. It's time to explore the neighboring islands—Jack Screw, the Secretaries, and Mowgali. We welcome absentee ownership. Fifty-two weeks a year they are parks for everyone to enjoy. A sort of noble communism. Yet I hesitate to trespass on a "one man's island." Like today, exploring seven-acre Mowgali, I felt uneasy—as if I were intruding on a private dream. To me, this is a far greater intrusion than invading someone's real estate.

There was no sign of life on Mowgali, but a trail marked by beach stones wound through the woods to a well among the cedars. In a nearby clearing, we stumbled onto the foundation timbers of a house, overgrown by salal and small hemlocks. The cooing of wild pigeons intensified the stillness, and the heaviness in our hearts of a dream cut short. By the time we had circled Mowgali's shore, it was nearly noon. We ate lunch on a white shell beach ringed by giant firs.

It was then we noticed the sign—For Sale—on a stunted juniper.

"Wonder how much," I said.

"More than we've got."

"For a down payment?"

Jeanne smiled knowingly. "You'd buy a rock if it was surrounded by water."

Islomania runs in my blood. I would rather talk about islands than eat; would rather—and often do—think about islands than sleep. Even a scraggly tree-topped reef, I deem sacred. A large island is no better than a continent. "It has to be quite small," said D. H. Lawrence, "before it *feels* like an island." Small enough for the eye to know intimately every cove, fir, and glen. For one to know those secret places where, each spring, lady-slippers and camus lilies abound.

Islands resemble people. They can be brutal and kind, enchanting and ugly, adorable and dangerous. Without a good anchorage, the loveliest island—as one islander will bear witness—can be a heartless vixen on a stormy night. As a rule, one warms up to an island as one does to a stranger. Green and gently sloping shores with a sandy beach invite the eye like a friendly smile and a firm hand. You want to get better acquainted. The steep cliffs of Charles and Lizard islands make me want to go on by.

Like people, islands can be deceiving. At first sight years ago, Wallace gave me a sense of foreboding. The sandstone bluffs loomed up like fortress walls, and the boulder-strewn shoreline was cold and uninviting. I wondered how we'd get ashore. Then a cove opened and ushered us into a landlocked lagoon—like an emerald lake embedded in the forest that all but locked out the world.

Private islands over two hundred acres, I don't mind exploring. There seems a limit where a dream ends and ostentation begins. Islands like Parker, Moresby, and Samuel are too large to be loved (or utilized) by a single person. One can possess only what one loves. For love is a form of reciprocal intimacy. The only way to own an island is to live on it. In most cases, an island belongs to its caretaker more than to its actual owner.

Now that subdivision fever is spreading, large islands will no longer be the monopoly of one man. At times, the urge to sell part of ours is tempting, for Wallace falls close to two hundred acres—and I feel guilty that we can utilize only a fraction of it. But like the connoisseur millionaire, I am greedy. I rationalize that the island is a resort; that part of the year we share it with others. The other part—luckily, the longest—we hoard Wallace to ourselves.

A DARK, DRIZZLY DAY. The cove is as leaden and motionless as my thoughts. This afternoon we built a fire, the first since April, and watched the flames leap and glow. It warmed our spirits as well as the room.

Will writes: "You've been at it two years. Haven't you finished that saga yet?" I'm afraid not, Will. Only six chapters so far. It took a year to outline the story. Lord knows how long it will take to write it. I lack discipline, the flow of words. When I face a sheet of paper, everything coils up and stops inside. Words rarely come to fit my thoughts. Each sentence must be hammered out. My mind wanders. The inclination to read excites me more than to write. I indulge myself in long periods of gestation and reflection. As steeping increases the flavor of tea, so it increases the value of the written word. This is the excuse I give myself. But the fact remains, I am not a writer. My fanny is allergic to a chair, my den more often a prison than a joy. I am a *lover*. There are too many things I love and would rather do.

Writing should be the product of living, not made into a living. The books we like best are those that have been lived. The reward of reading them is that they read us—our thoughts, desires, and dreams. When one writes too much, one lives too little. How many persons with nothing to say go on writing books for the lack of courage to do anything else? There is no dearth of cleverness, of brilliance, but so little excellence—that rare quality of thought and expression from rich and noble minds. What a difference between books by mere writers and those by vital people! Do we not thirst for more Saint-Exupérys? More spiritual harvests like *Gift from the Sea?* Heartfelt, soul-tickling adventures in living like *The Egg and I?* "For writing"—that crusty old pro Somerset Maugham admitted—"the important thing is less richness of material than richness of personality." One needs to perfect not one's craft so much as one's self. To create anything of value, we must *be* something of value. What is needed is not better writing, but better men writing.

OCTOBER BRINGS US mallards, grebes, and loons, also the fishpacker with six months' supply of gas and oil. This morning the wharf groaned with 350-pound drums, and I groaned too, rolling them up the gangway. Tonight I feel a vast ease such as the squirrel must feel with a full storehouse of fir cones. Bring on your winter!

Oh, but wait! There's no antifreeze in the launch, the water pump hasn't been drained, nor the begonias brought into the root cellar. You can't postpone things, else you pay dearly for your laziness. I am again reminded of the squirrel. How hard he works all summer to keep himself all winter. But isn't our mink the wiser? Perhaps the happier? He does not spoil his summers with toil. He lives only for the day, the seashore supplying a ready dinner. He enjoys life too much to hibernate. Yet isn't he missing something?

For my part, I need the joy of anticipation—and need to dream. Wouldn't the continuous chore of obtaining food every waking moment prove monotonous? How wonderful it is just to sit before the fire on a wintry day, knowing the woodshed and larder are full, with nothing to worry about but the characters in your book?

Much as I admire the hearty mink—his dual nature as both land and sea animal—I must go along with the squirrel. He can look out at the snow, like me, then settle back and dream it's summer.

Dreams are very real things. All achievement begins with them. They are the radar of the mind, links to the future. For it's in our dreams that we first come to know how to live.

FIRST FOGGY MORNING. The crows are upset; their raucous cries shred the air. Will they make their daily flight to Salt Spring, or be stuck here to heckle us all day? Already the orchard is taking the brunt of their anger. In for coffee, I exclaimed, "If the fog doesn't lift, there won't be a king left on the trees." We banged the dishpan—and off they flew, screaming in the silver haze.

I write to Anne, an editor at Johns Hopkins Press:

Yes, Anaïs Nin's Diary *is terribly soul-searching. But, my God—what brutal honesty! How rare it is these days. It's easier to flee into fiction, camouflage ourselves with immunity in the characters of a novel. Another quality I admire is that her intellectuality has warmth. Gandhi once stated that what saddened him the most was the hardheartedness of the educated. He's right, of course. We school the mind, but fail to school the heart. No wonder the youth of today yearns for a life of noble savagery. The result is the drift toward an affectionless society, epitomized by "playing it cool"—being unconcerned and unaffected, traits which more closely resemble a computer than a human being. Is not indifference—the cold withdrawal of human feeling—one of the most persistent tragedies of our time?*

I wonder, Anne, if we have not forgotten what it means to be human. Life is not a thing of knowing. It is a thing of feeling. We must feel what we know. As Pascal said, "The emotions have a logic which reason does not fathom." It is not the intellect but the heart that makes us human. Never has mankind held so much knowledge with so little wisdom, held so much power with so little understanding. "Everything we know," said Valéry, "which is to say, everything we can do, has finally turned against what we are."

Ours is a heroless age from which only the hero can extricate us. Not the technician or the specialist, but he who would make Man his cause—"the measure of all things." Where, even remotely, is there a Camus or a Gide

—a directeur de conscience *for the young and the hopeful?*
Men who are, in some sense, exemplary, and incarnate the
moral-spiritual issues of the times; who live by their visions
as well as write them; and who, in this morass of technology
called "progress," can show us how to be?

THE MITCHELLS dropped by yesterday in their new boat. It's
one of those triple-hulled affairs—forty by twenty, glistening
white, and speedy as a dolphin under sail. They've sold their
house on Salt Spring and are now living aboard—all six of
them (four small girls)! Quite a boat—just don't know what
to make of it. But I admire their pluck for doing what *they*
want to do.

MUSHROOMS! We've never seen so many. They litter the forest
floor like bands of tunicked dwarfs, from the size of a dishpan
to that of the smallest fingernail. I have been Gulliver all
afternoon, in fantasyland, on hands and knees with my camera. Their domes are oriental palaces, and blades of grass are
surrounding forests. Jeanne is cataloging each species, learning their names, and collecting some in a bowl. I felt a bit
apprehensive.

"When is a mushroom not a toadstool?" I asked.

She grinned. "When it's too late."

In no small way, I have been successful in enjoying my
ignorance. There are still many common plants, flowers, and
birds I am unable to identify, for I have a distinct laziness
about labeling things. This causes me no worry, as I am not
out really to learn them.

Nature to me is like my wife. Her charm is in her mystery.
When I think I know her is when I know her least. For if I
seek to fathom her thought, she merely presents me with another. Her disposition is never dull, as her seasons are so
delightfully intermixed. A single day encompasses a year of
weather. There is warmth in her silence as in her voice; beauty

MUSHROOMS—OR TOADSTOOLS?

in her stillness as in her movement—for June constantly abides in her heart.

In the sheathing of love, who is the most delighted?

How often when the day has no flavor we depend on sex to give it seasoning.

IN THE WOODS at dusk I think of the clogged freeways—the fumes and the fret of the weary homeward bound. Another day sold . . . the life not lived, the dreams not won. I feel truly blessed. Where others wish for the quitting whistle, I wish for a longer day so that when night comes I do not feel cheated by the hours. Would to heaven we could exist without sleep—what men we could become!

What I want most is not happiness but *aliveness.* To see, feel, and expand. To complete all that structure within that begs finishing. What mansions we are! Why do we hole up in one room?

These mornings I feel more comfortable with the door open. Not enough of the forest can enter through the window.

Ecstasy. Words that tumble onto the page in such torrents that I can't wait to see what I've said.

ON WEDNESDAY I borrowed the money from Lester and bought Mowgali Island. A steal at twelve hundred dollars. I have kept it a secret from Jeanne while preparing my defense. Its resale could solve many of our problems.

MORE COLD, CHILLING FOG. All day the island has been a prison to the crows—and to Jeanne. I can stand the clamor in the trees, but not the clamor in the house. "Wouldn't you know it," Jeanne groaned, "just when I wanted to go shopping. Blast it! You can't plan anything on an island."

She had a point. To be happy on an island you have to face the fact that appointments are made to be broken. Doctors, dentists, and hairdressers grow to hate you.

You and ferryboats go by different times.

You run out of ways to fix noodles.

You can never dine out, or expect company without the risk of having house guests for days—even weeks.

You are constantly repairing worn-out machinery (for which you can't get parts).

Your hands are always grimy, seldom empty, and your back is always bent.

You get atrociously set in your ways.

You don't want to go anywhere. You get out of touch, slovenly, and self-centered.

You moan in despair, "Nothing comes easy on an island" —be it digging a simple ditch, raising children, money—or leeks.

You become dewy-eyed toward humanity, wanting to rush up to every stranger and hug him—even the mutual fund salesman who wanders by.

You shop in fear—that a tap has been left running, or the wind is ripping the wash to bits.

The city is organized chaos—you're apt to panic in the elevator, or pick up every virus within a mile; and nothing works or fits that you bring back from town.

If you are a kind, generous, good-natured person, the island will change you into a mean, selfish clam-hater. After a succession of gloomy winter days, you'll feel like giving it to the first Indian who paddles in. Yet you are terribly fickle. The moment the sun sneaks out and the cove glitters among the firs, you wouldn't sell it for a million dollars.

MY NIGHTS ARE given to study. But the more I learn, the less sure I am of what I know. I devour one book after another, one author after another, more possessed by pursuit than the quarry. I thirst for light, like the fir forest, the days being but ways I climb to seek it. Everything in the forest seems to strive for light. Plants, vines, birds, reptiles. Some people are like salal. They hug the base of firs, dwarfed and spindly, content to accept small rays from above. Yet each plant and each man has his place—all are humus that nourishes the common whole. Where some dig ditches, others climb aloft—design and create, thus giving labor to the vast family of man. One mind creates a thousand jobs. One idea sets a million free. For the lot of many always resides in the lot of the few. Where tens of thousands rest at the end of the day, another continues to labor. To spiral upward—to live on the stretch. It is from the lumber of these lofty firs that civilization builds and expands. "Only stretched souls make music," said Hoffer, those passionate few who are not satisfied to be what they are.

Einstein's advice to young people:
"Try not to become a man of success, but rather to become a man of value."

My memory frightens me. This morning, I couldn't remember what I had written yesterday. I seem to forget everything—the day, the time, the month. Even my lists. "Everything," Jeanne laughs, "except what to do in bed."

Each morning, like Wallie, I go out to sniff the world as if it had been re-created overnight.

WE HAVE BEEN picking apples all afternoon. Kings are good keepers—firm, tangy, and ruby red. Davey shook the highest limbs where the ladder didn't reach, and we caught the fruit in a sheet. After sorting out the imperfects—some for juice and some for the sheep—we stored fourteen boxes. The pungent smell of the root cellar is intoxicating.

Of all my habits, none is more habitual than "an apple (or two) a day." Failing that, a cold glass of apple juice. I am glad science has proved that the apple, which caused such a fuss in the Garden of Eden, does "keep the doctor away." (A substance in pectin keeps us healthier by reducing our cholesterol.) Eve can't be blamed for taking the first bite. An apple holds life. At this rate, I should reach the year 2000!

LIKE AN AGED MAN, October passed on. November mourns, as rain clouds hang like silver gauze among the firs. Every fir needle drips. Everything is bent and weeping. Even the air is so damp it is an effort to breathe. The earth oozes, leaves

JEANNE AND KIKI AT APPLE HARVESTTIME

are soggy, and puddles have swollen into lakes. The island won't hold any more. From every nook and crevice, water gurgles, gushes, and tumbles into the cove.

The fireplace is our furnace. It goes all day. Its sound and scent enliven the warmth in every room. Jeanne is the thermostat. I just try to keep the woodbox full.

IN THE MAIL today, a heartwarming letter:

> *Dear Dave & Jeanne: I cannot begin to tell you folks what a wonderful time we all had on your island last summer. It may interest you to know that I've sold my business and bought tickets to take my wife and me around the world. When we come back, I've got my eye on a few acres in the San Juans. I'm going to take root and LIVE. Yes—I'll hunt, fish, and farm and really enjoy the hobby we once had: antiques.*
>
> *I regret that I didn't wise up sooner. But I am only 55 and I've got years to go. Seeing what you have done, I know now we can't find happiness when we're out to conquer the world. We can gain it only by carving a small niche somewhere and making it fruitful with our own spirit. Kindest regards to all.*
>
> *Donald Dirkson.*

November's joy is purely a personal thing. At last we can leave a tap running without a wince—strike up the washing machine, flush the sea water from the toilet, soak the potted plants, and bathe gloriously under the shower without thought of the well. Life is returning to normal. "Now," Jeanne remarked, "I don't feel guilty every time I wash my hair."

I am wary of writers who are too nimble with words. Prose is not a song. It is not meant to dance, but to walk. Thought must have a chance to engulf and lap up the word.

Time to digest its meaning. The styles I like best—those of Gide and Thoreau—are translucent. Simple yet rich, meaty but not sententious.

Creative processes have much in common. What fun it is to let yourself go, on paper, in the garden—or in bed!

THIS MORNING Jeanne and Davey ran off to Victoria. I kept banging away on the infernal machine. Hours slipped by. Not until four o'clock did I realize the time. How keenly my mind ticked—the pages I dashed off! I must skip lunch more often. "Food for thought?"—I should say not!

I have made a momentous discovery. The cove has an echo. By the crooked madrona, I stood in awe—much like Crusoe—hearing my voice returned to me. It instilled a certain strangeness, for the voice sounded like someone else—far older, more knowledgeable, and profound. I listened for a time, amazed by its authority. I uttered foolish thoughts— they came back as wise ones. If only the same would happen on paper.

I write standing, rewrite at the desk. The legs of the mind become cramped when I sit for long. My thoughts go to sleep if I don't stretch and move about.

LAST NIGHT I finished Collin's partial manuscript, *The Riotous Ark*. Delightful. Even better than I expected. This morning I wrote:

> *Your main problem, Collin, is cohesion. No matter how charming, funny, or thought-provoking, anecdotes cannot stand alone without a unifying influence. In a word, you lack a theme. A string to set off your pearls.*

For years it has been my feeling that Anne Lindbergh jotted her thoughts in notebooks. Finally one day she had enough for a book. How was she to prevent them from being a collection of dry philosophic essays? She needed a thread for her pearls of wisdom. On the seashore, picking up shells, it came to her. The lives of certain sea creatures and human life had traits in common. The result—her classic Gift from the Sea.

If you have not done so, you should put a theme on paper. First in a paragraph, then in a sentence. It will help you to cut and edit. Make your chapters prove your theme. What is your theme? I don't know exactly, but I think I know what it should be (though you might not agree): Love for animals determines one's success in selling them. As for your crisis—if a man pulls you out, it will not be as effective as if a dog did. Your intense love of animals is the most powerful quality of your book. If you allow your devotion, your faith in them, to resolve the climax, that will be all the plot you need. Hook the reader first; then follow with your episodes, keeping them well mixed and promising. Then let him off the hook in the final chapter. Just a thought. Hope it's worth something.

THERE HAS BEEN an alarming drop in the keg of nails. Davey is building a raft on the beach. We are studying his progress from the kitchen window. "I don't want anyone around," he had made it plain, "telling me what to do." Now we are quite excited. He's determined to launch it at high tide tonight.

"Think it'll float?" Jeanne asked.

Recalling our first attempt, I smiled. "He can't do any worse than we did."

Morning is my most prized possession. I stand over it

DAVEY BUILDS A RAFT

like a tyrant, while the afternoon stands over me. Better I write, better the axe flies. On a good day, I figure, five pages is equal to a cord of wood.

Strive for this: The stillness that will let you be aware of your aliveness, so that you may feel the aliveness in others, and the growth all round you.

As life evolved from the sea, all flights of my mind begin in the blood. The woodpile stirs a tempest that fires two furnaces; just as a pick loosens rocks from the hillside, so it causes an avalanche in my mind. The intellect covets what is discovered through sweat. My brain is a sluice gate, ready to grab every thought that darts out.

This evening Davey, all ajoy, towed his raft around to the wharf.

THE LAST FEW NIGHTS, I have been reading Hoffer. He is a rough diamond, like Whitman, in that he combines the characteristics of a Concord philosopher with those of a Maine backwoodsman. I admire his profundity and incisiveness, but his naïveté, prejudices, and arch-conservatism irritate me. The perfect example of the danger of being self-taught! However, we should be grateful. The man is so much of the earth and truth and wonderful nitty-gritty that you have to love him for what he is. For ultimately, I believe, we are all self-taught, and the creation of one's self is indeed the highest art.

I am always contemplating a nobler life than I am ever able to attain. Some nights I bathe, spruce up, and commence to write with the expectation of being visited by distinguished thoughts. Surprisingly, I am not too often disappointed with the company.

SAWING WOOD THE HARD WAY

ANOTHER EXQUISITE September day. The sea is a mirror, the distant islands are hazy and limpid like a Japanese watercolor. There's hardly a sound, just the crackling of madrona bark, the buzz of a housefly. I want to do nothing except loaf. But the inner man says, "Get after those weeds in the garden, split those rounds for the fireplace."

I write to Max:

Your remarks about women *have overtones of Scho-penhauer.* (His essay on the subject is priceless.) *But don't let Mildred get you down. There's a bit of a bitch in any good woman. After all, what don't we owe to Xanthippe for driving Socrates into the streets!*

By all means, do that humorous article you mentioned. You have a gift for satire. It could start you rolling. Send it to the editor of the Vancouver Times. *He's always looking for fresh talent. But don't wait. Tackle it before your interest cools. Do you keep a thought-book? If not, you should. I write constantly in mine. It's like self-exploration for hidden stores. Writing is a spiritual purification—the distillation of one's best. (Poor Jeanne—how often she is faced with only the dregs!)*

I sometimes grow disheartened that the resort has deprived me of so much writing time . . . that I have produced so little. Yet did not Thoreau's skill in pencil-making sharpen his sentences? Spinoza's lens-grinding give clarity to his thought? Longfellow's love and care of his roses enhance the beauty of his poetry? Our work is worth only as much as we are worth. Oh, what a long way I have to go!

Between "deluges" I am making a flagstone path around the house, and finishing the rock wall at the wharf. Funny, I'd rather face a bag of cement than a

SIGNS AT THE WHARF

blank sheet of paper. It seems happiness eludes me unless my hands are dirty.

Let me know what's ticking in that Teutonic brain— your beefs, loves, dreams, anything but politics. It's a man's inner rule that interests me.

IT'S AMAZING how much goes on down at the wharf. In summer it's crowded with people, poodles, and boats. Now it's populated with ducks, gulls, herons, and crows. Only an otter dozes lazily in the sun. Wallie considers the floats part of his domain. He dashes down, as in summer, to scare off those who do not pay moorage—the Scotsman in him!—a pretty sight, his tail arched and long elegant nose raised defiantly in the morning sun. The heron squawks, rising clumsily, and the otter snarls like an angry cat as he plunges from sight. Ducks whisk away in a clatter of wings, while crows light among the madronas and clang nosily at such an unruly disturbance.

Every moment something is going on. Mink and spider crabs feed on the mussels that cling to the float logs. Teredos work around the clock, spewing a constant stream of digested wood. Like powder puffs, sea anemones expand and contract their silky mouths. Barnacles fan the sea. In the moonlight, seals sleep huddled together, the stillness broken by their snores. Dogfish fin, hunting for prey. Buffleheads feast on pileworms; cormorants sit stiffly atop pilings like hooded monks, as Kiki, with feline patience, stalks a rat cleaning up tidbits left by the mink.

A SOUTHEASTERLY GALE. All night the wind roared among the firs and waves pounded the shores, as if to wrench the island from its mooring. Result—another drizzly day. Tides were too high for clams, so we had stew for dinner. Davey looked at his plate. "Gee, Mom—not again."

Think with courage. The more you qualify, the more diluted the thought. Try to eliminate: "it seems," "appears," "possibly." How well Goethe puts it: "If I am to listen to another man's opinion, he must express it positively. I have enough of the problematical in myself."

I am not especially bright or witty—or gifted; and a poor memory makes it a struggle to accomplish a thing. But as an enjoyer, I am a master; I can stand up to the greatest men. I enjoy Plato as well as *Playboy,* Debussy as well as the Beatles, Van Gogh as well as Grandma Moses. My soul gravitates toward the best of each kind. In Vic's barn, I stand in reverence. Its dome of handhewn fir beams and airy loft filled with meadow gold are no less beautiful to me than the Sistine Chapel.

STILL POURING. Raindrops squirm and wiggle on the windowpanes like restless children in a classroom.

To live in this country, your lungs must be gills. The air is two parts liquid, one part mist. The ground like the sky flows, rushes, and drums. Dampness seeps into everything. Windows weep, doors stick, drawers won't open. The good nature in human nature becomes all burr and self-grinding.

All day lost in the underbrush of wooden thoughts.

I WROTE VERY LITTLE this morning. Oh, this inertia! If only I could rid myself of such complete absorption in books. Why is my will so weak? My material is abundant; our Mr. and Mrs. Crusoe story is a *natural.* I must impose myself on it, pull all the pieces together into a harmonizing mosaic. What is talent without force of character to bring it to fruition?

I must confess the nakedness of this truth: I have taken too much of Renard without adding enough of myself. Ironically, he himself observed, "How hard we work before we help ourselves, quite simply, to our own originality."

Davey rushed in the door.

"Papa, you can come out. The sky is empty now."

WHITE FROST. Innumerable spider webs among the salal—necklaces spread at random through the forest. I hurry for the camera. It's the only time the spider's trap is naked to its prey—and my lens.

SPIDER WEB AMID THE SALAL

*

A discouraging day. The westerly gale knocked the gangway off its runners, the launch sprang a leak, and now this evening the lights began to flicker. How chores rob me of creativity. No wonder my thoughts are so erratic. My mind is never free of some urgent duty. A time will come when I must simplify.

"Funny thing," I remarked to Jeanne this evening while we were having our bedtime tea. "The Gulf Islands really do not exist—there are no gulfs in British Columbia."

"That's strange. Perhaps you can do something."

"Like what?"

"Write the editor of *Driftwood* and suggest a name. He might go for the idea."

I went to the den and stuck a sheet of paper in the typewriter.

Dear Mr. Fisher:

I am sick of hearing Americans refer to our islands as the Canadian San Juans. Yet what else can they call them? Our islands have no real name. The Gulf Islands cannot be found on any map or chart, for none of the waters around here is named the gulf of anything (not since the Gulf of Georgia became the Straits of Georgia way back in the 19th century). Besides, why should we hang onto an "old-time handle" that is now inaccurate, misleading, and devoid of geographical significance?

Let's give our islands a genuine title, a title that means something, a title that does justice to their incomparable beauty. For what else have they? Think of the Thousand Islands—what beauty and romance that name conjures! The Hawaiian Islands . . . the Bahamas . . . the Canaries all designate a definite place; all the names are unique and colorful, all are in the atlas. Our islands deserve a better fate than obscurity. What a challenge it

*would be to put them "on the map." Let's get the ball
rolling and give them a proper name.*

I submit the name Princess Islands.

*It ties in geographically (Princess Margaret's Island) and historically (Princess ship era), and the name
has beauty, dignity, and color. What more can you ask?*

I HAVE CONSTRUCTED a bathroom bookshelf. (If I had been
more inclined toward constipation, I might have become a
scholar.) On the throne this morning, the first sentence I read,
Camus asked, "Is there a tragic dilettantism?" I wonder.

Winter

He who has never seen himself
surrounded on all sides by the sea can never
possess an idea of the world, and of his relation
to it.

—Goethe

AT COVE EDGE AFTER A SNOW

IT'S DECEMBER and dark now at three thirty. We eat dinner on the card table before the fire. Afterward, we gather round the burning logs, read, and sip cups of tea to the strains of Dvořák. A game of Old Maid soon entices Davey off to bed. While Jeanne sews, I read aloud fresh pages of my saga, for an inkling as to their quality. She is an uncompromising critic. Too often a man falls in love with his Pygmalion and cannot see her blemishes. The hours fly by so fast we seldom complete a game of chess.

Before bedtime, we inspect the wharf and boat and make sure the tide has not made off with our beachcombings. One more cup of tea; then the last switch turns the generator off. Only the moonglow and channel blinker push back the darkness. As I fall asleep I remember Mrs. Barnes, who asked, "What do you do with yourself on those long winter nights?"

I am still reading Gide's *Journals*. Fascinating. He has all the contradictions of genius. On page 137, he says, "Man achieves nothing worthwhile without constraint"; then, on

137

page 354, he adds, "Some people work over themselves to obtain unity of their person. I let myself go." Nevertheless, he amazes me. Not since Montaigne has anyone revealed to me the depths of my inner self with more lucidity and so little pain.

ON WEDNESDAY the first letters arrived in response to my ad for Mowgali Island in *The Wall Street Journal*. I couldn't contain my excitement—or my secret.

I tossed the mail on the table. "Here's the winter parka you've been wanting."

Jeanne read the letters carefully.

"You crazy man!" Her face broke into a grin. "You shouldn't have. Who's going to buy an island in the dead of winter?"

I grinned back. "Want to bet?"

She shook her head sheepishly.

LORD, HOW IT RAINS! It's like living downstream from a waterfall. This wet and gloom, I have developed a partial immunity to. But poor Jeanne—her spirits ebb and flow with the sun. This afternoon I found her disconsolate beside the sewing machine. "It's too dark, Dave." She raised a puckered face. "It's too dark to do anything. When do you suppose the sun will shine again?"

I turned on a light. "Isn't that better?"

"We shouldn't," she protested. "It wastes gas."

"Doesn't matter"—I kissed her lips—"if it makes you smile."

What I fear most is emptiness. Abatement of soul. The paralyzing halt of vital juices. When I find myself in this void, I wonder if I shall recover. It wastes me . . . makes me irritable. I am more vegetable than animal. To convince myself that I pulsate, I wager my manliness. The sexual act regenerates me.

LAST NIGHT during the storm there was a knock on the door. With a sense of foreboding, I got up from the table.

"My boat threw a rod," said the stranger, out of breath. "She's anchored among the reefs off the north end. Have you a phone?"

He was a short stocky fellow, gray at the temples, wearing jeans and a blazer. The way the wind was howling, I knew he must have had a terrible ordeal, yet as he stood there soaked and shivering, he didn't seem unduly upset. Under the circumstances, only an Englishman could be so self-collected. I remembered having seen him years before in Chemainus operating a water taxi.

We explained the button system on the radiophone. His wife couldn't hear. "I'm on Wallace Island, luv. The motor went. You know how I've been expectin' it to. Call one of the tugs. Have them come right away."

He released the button.

"Where are you, Charlie?" his wife came on.

"Wallace Island. The Conovers'."

"I'll get one of the boys. Do they know where to go?"

"Yes, the middle bay. There's a light. Don't worry, luv. Everything is all right."

I couldn't help admiring the man. His boat was in great danger—the tug might be hours in coming—yet he did not want to involve me in its rescue. Where his boat was, off Chivers Point, with the dark, the reefs, and rough seas, I was not keen to go after it. Then I put myself in his shoes. In those waters, a tug wouldn't chance a rescue till morning. His boat, like mine, was his livelihood.

"You'd better have some coffee," Jeanne said to him, "while I get you dry things."

"No," I said. "We'd better go. No anchor will hold in that spot." The white shell bottom held little gripping power. "Put on another plate, darling. We'll be back in a bit."

Charlie Rojack was a true seaman. I could feel it in his calm as the launch breasted the waves, the confidence with which he wiped the steamy windows. He was not as tense as I felt. Ahead, the spotlight grazed the whitecaps as my eyes strained for drift and deadheads. In the stern were the anchor and a coiled towline.

"There she is," Charlie pointed. "Over there." A white boat tossed and bobbed behind the rocks, the seas breaking over them and swinging it barely a dozen feet from shore.

"We'll have to round the reefs, Charlie . . . work up between them and the island. There's a shallow channel. We can't get to her any other way."

The launch chugged valiantly ahead, the heavy seas grumbling in the darkness. Moments later we skirted the chain of reefs that parallel Wallace, and were creeping alongshore. Overhead, swaying fir branches nearly touched the boat. Off to port, rocks raised their heads in the surging waves. I felt a chill sweep my spine. The fathometer registered seven . . . five . . . four feet. From the backlash against shore, waves exploded around us. We rolled and tossed. It was like edging our way through a mine field.

Fifty yards ahead the water taxi pitched and heaved in the blur of the windshield. I could hardly keep the spot on it, and I worried how to get a line aboard. It was impossible to come alongside—to risk the safety of the boat. Charlie had the answer.

"Slacken the throttle," he hollered, a boat's length off. "We'll use the anchor line for the tow."

As we came abreast, his pike hooked the rope. The next instant I heard the clatter of chain aboard. "Okay!" he yelled. "Let's get out of here."

We started back, hugging the reefs to keep the tow from

striking shore. Nose into the wind, we inched crab-fashion along the island. The motor pounded in my ears. I felt even more fearful. Charlie's boat was a slim, sweet twenty-foot cabin craft. On board was mail, express parcels, 120 loaves of bread. Then we saw open water, the lumpy seas blurred by the drizzle of rain. Never did a house light seem so welcome, shining like a star off the starboard bow.

By means of ethics I seek to improve myself, to police my nature. I make strict rules and attempt to follow them, but my nature always wins out. For weeks now I have strived to free myself of these wretched cigars. Yet for each one I promised to give up, I have smoked three more. Funny— the hardest task is to do what is "good" for us.

I am not a joiner. I could never give an institution, party, or organization my full support, for there are always in them elements which are not my own, and the surest way to end up with a closed mind is to become an ardent supporter. Only a free force can act totally in *man's* behalf in a world of tied forces. To do so, one should be uncommitted as far as possible—to belong on the occasion, not beyond the occasion. Such a man, visualized so ably by John Fowles in *The Aristos*, "needs no uniform, no symbols; his ideas are his uniform, his actions are his symbols."

Is God on the way out? Or, is man on the way down?

A MORNING SO GRAY and grizzly the crows have gone back to bed. In winter the days are but shorter nights.

I am disturbed by Joseph Wood Krutch's statement that Thoreau has been "increasingly admired without exercising an increasing influence." Tommyrot! How can a person genuinely admire someone without being susceptible to his influence? Thoreau, in particular, who impels self-action, self-reform. He was gloriously provincial, but by his example he injected something precious into the mainstream of history which is still nourishing the human consciousness. Gandhi and Martin Luther King hailed him as supremely contemporary. How many people, for instance, has he not inspired to throw off the yoke of materialism? To "simplify"? I am a Thoreauvian, by heart and by deed—and if he reaches even me, pray tell what other corners of the globe have not felt the influence of his abrasive spirit? One traveler reports he could buy more different editions of *Walden* in Tokyo than in New York City!

Thoreau's influence is greatest where it is least readily seen—in the private sensibility. He acts as a catalyst by invoking response to our innermost selves. He arouses our sense of wonder, of the privilege and excitement of life. "To read Thoreau," said J. Donald Adams, "is to realize how many parts of us are but half alive." For he lived to an extraordinary degree with all his senses, intellect, and feeling. The danger is that his sentences have such beauty, crispness, and compelling power that our lives may be changed by them.

MORE RAIN, HEAVY SEAS—a week now without mail or groceries. Nothing but gloom. "What this island needs is a bridge," Jeanne declared, frantically trying to find a cigarette butt.

I am beginning to believe her. Almost.

Nothing convinces me more of the lightness of my mind than my taste in music. Bach and Beethoven do not play for me. In the record stand, their albums sit like two old maids at a dance. Perhaps it's the weather that makes me ignore them, prefer the exuberant strains of Chopin's *Polonaise* or the gay-hearted melodies of Leroy Anderson.

Tonight, as the phonograph went on with the generator,

Jeanne remarked, "It's a good thing we don't have city power. Our records would be worn out." All except poor Bach and Beethoven.

I am atrociously impractical. Instead of buying new tires, I buy used books and recordings I am unable to appreciate or understand, because those tastes I respect assure me of their goodness. Miserly, I lay up future stores of enjoyment.

THE WESTERLY WIND brought a shoreful of bark, which we've been gathering to help fill the cavern in the woodshed. Split wood doesn't last as long as or give near the heat of bark. Barometer is rising, temperature has fallen—a chilly thirty degrees tonight.

Davey is lying on the sofa, gazing dreamily at the shadows on the well. "Someday I want my own island."

"For goodness sake," Jeanne replied, "what's wrong with this one?"

"It's too crowded, Mom. Someone's always watching me. Haven't you wanted to get away from it all?"

I have titled Chapter Five "Desperate Voyage." It is symbolic, now that I look back, of our whole adventure. I've rewritten it nine times. Still not satisfied!

ALL DAY I HAVE been struggling with the significance of Plato's remark: "For a soul to know itself, it must contemplate another." He means, I think, simply that only through others do we come to know ourselves. Man's eternal quest is for relatedness. To grow in learning, to open up to the world, as Gide says, we must truly find those to whom we are akin. I recognize a brother in Keats, Goethe, and Thoreau; a cousin in Arnold, Montaigne, and Emerson. They fill an obscure emptiness so that I may become.

*

Though Jeanne does not agree, I believe the final test of a good meal is the dessert. I grew up with a sweet tooth. It still nags me. Jeanne has no problem when I fix the desserts —only my waistline. My latest concoction (I feel my way as I go) is banana custard. I use six eggs, sometimes eight; one banana, sometimes two. A dash of saccharin instead of sugar. I love it fresh from the oven—warm and velvety. Consistency is the thing. I like "body" in cakes and custard, as I like "substance" in a man. What is a cookie without the crunch?

I applaud this resolution of Cyril Connolly's: "Never again make any concession to the 99 percent of you which is like everybody else at the expense of the 1 percent which is unique."

STEAK AND MUSHROOMS tonight. This morning Mowgali sold to the first viewer—a jovial Mr. Hall, who flew up from Tacoma. In spite of the rain, it was "love at first sight." We are quite excited—without a quibble he wrote us a check for $6,500. No longer do we need to hang on by a tenuous thread.

"What shall we do with the money?" Jeanne asked breathlessly.

I was one step ahead.

"Build a cottage, and save the rest for Davey's education." I flicked the check with a grin. "You know, don't you, this could eventually put us in the income tax bracket?"

We roared.

"WHEN WE LOVE," writes Samuel Butler in his notebooks, "we draw what we love closer to us; when we hate a thing we fling it away from us. All disruption and dissolution is a mode of hating; and all that we call affinity is a mode of loving."

We can condition our affinity—not with the mind, which is easy, but with the heart. Mrs. Adams has her own recipe:

"I try to single out the thing I like most about a person," she says, "and I try always to think of that. It's surprising how it works." Love begins as we begin to overlook.

Bear in mind Rod McKuen's words "It is not how we love or who we love but that we love."

WE HAVE JUST returned from a shopping spree in Victoria. Wallie and Kiki greeted us jubilantly at the dock. It took us an hour—fumbling for parcels in the dark—and two cartloads to unload the launch. The only thing we picked up that didn't cost anything is sore feet.

On the ferry, this note:
In the city I feel deprived of my natural wealth. I become all eye. Half my faculties go begging, become even unwanted. The sense of smell, hearing, feeling—all suffer malnutrition from ocular despotism. Invaded by the external, I find my inner self emptied, transformed into a gateway through which a throng of objects come and go.

AS JEANNE READ the letter, she cried, "Mother's coming for Christmas. She's leaving L.A. tomorrow."
They say there are no two people alike. I can well believe it, for Alice is cut from the rarest mold. A small, gray-haired creature with doelike eyes, she has the vitality of a young sea captain who has taken command of a newly launched ship. Her candor is her charm. She not only says what she thinks, but she never stops to think what she says. Or, for that matter, knows what she'll do next. She tells everybody she's going to Arizona, the land of her dreams, for the winter. Come December, we get a postcard from Juneau, saying Alaska is more beautiful than she had ever believed.
We never know *how* or *when* Alice will arrive—much less, when she'll depart. Once she pulled into the harbor on a

fishboat. The next time, in a floatplane. She even hitched a ride from Victoria with a road contractor. The only time I've seen her speechless was when, at Fernwood, she saw "Danger —High Explosives—Keep at a Distance" on the truck as it disappeared up the hill.

"Getting ready for Mother," Jeanne declares, "is harder than preparing for winter." Kiki is booted out the window (Alice is allergic to cats, Democrats, and dust); the house is thoroughly GI'd and atomized with pine scent—to forestall the complaint "Good Lord! Every room smells of garlic." Closets and dressers are disgorged to hold her wardrobe; subversive literature, such as *The Affluent Society* and *Profiles in Courage,* is shoved under the couch, and the photo of Ike that she sent is dug out and hung on the wall.

Dear Alice. I really love her. Her suggestions can be so helpful. The Indian dugout canoe, for instance, she said would make a wonderful flower box. I nearly slipped a disk hauling it up the bank, through the clump of willows, and onto the lawn. Then direct orders came for special soil—one part this, one part that, with a liberal application of cow manure, peat moss, and every available starfish. She volunteered the seed, a packet of nasturtiums. They grew like wildfire. So did the army of termites. When the leaves were the size of lily pads, the deer came down one night and ate the works. The termites ate the rest. But—bless her heart—we still love Alice.

"The house is so small," Jeanne worried. "If only we had a guest room. Oh, well, Mother will just have to sleep on the couch." She turned to me. "We could give her . . ."

"Oh, no," I spurted, pulling her leg. "Last time Alice had the bedroom I thought she'd never leave."

"That's not so," Jeanne protested. "You know how squeamish Mother is about boats. The channel was just too rough."

I put my arm around her. "I know."

*

ALICE'S FAMOUS CANOE

In looking through the latest issue of *Archaeology* (the subject fascinates me), I am appalled by its dullness. I wish to heaven someone would put a little life into those ancient ruins!

The Mediterranean—not the Atlantic Ocean—I feel, holds the secret of the lost continent of Atlantis. I have read every source book, studied every suggestion as to its site, only to fall back on the common assumption that, like a lost shoe or hat, it will invariably be found where we least suspect —right under our noses.

A WINTER STROLL

TODAY WE BUNDLED UP and went out to look for a Christmas tree. With literally thousands to choose from, the decision finally became impossible for Jeanne and me. However, only one tree held Davey's heart—at the corner of the meadow, a bushy nine-foot fir.

"It's too large," Jeanne said. "Our trimmings will never do."

"That's okay, Mom. We'll make some. That 'loom-num' stuff you use will work swell."

After several abortive attempts to get it in the door, it now stands majestically where the living room used to be.

My bookshelves contain all my unpublished works. For the books I love to read are those I wish I had written.

If only *we* could lose our hearts instead of our heads!

Nietzsche comforts me: "Many a man fails to become a thinker for the sole reason his memory is too good." (I love that boy!)

ON A CHRISTMAS CARD from Charlie were the words:

> Without the knowledge of longitude
> When drifting to your isle
> I send the deepest gratitude
> With gladness in my smile

Toward five o'clock Jeanne came down to the wharf just as I finished the last tier of the rock retaining wall. "It's lovely, Dave." Her eyes surveyed the forty-foot structure. "The circular sweep, the joints—everything. What a difference it makes to the approach. Won't Mother be amazed?"

RAW AND WINDY this morning, with flurries of snow. My frostbitten toes are tucked under Wallie, who sleeps beneath the desk. Oh, if only I could relax as he does! The Puritan strain persists: The moment I do nothing, I worry time's being wasted.

This afternoon Alice arrived at Fernwood in a freight truck. When the driver opened the tailgate, I understood the reason why.

"Don't look so shocked, Big Boy," she said with a grin. "I'm staying only a week. The trunks and boxes are for storage while I go on another trip."

The channel was choppy, and the thunderous exhaust from the staggering load minimized conversation. Through it all, Alice stoically gripped her seat in unaccustomed silence. At the landing, we waited expectantly for some sign of surprise. At last, as we pushed the cart up the path, we heard a pale voice say, "The place does look different."

ON THE HUGE, brightly wrapped box next to the Christmas tree was the tag: "To Jeanne from Santa, with love."

"Shall I?" Jeanne's eyes danced.

I nodded.

She tore off the wrapper eagerly. "A TV," she gasped. "Oh, you shouldn't have, Dave."

"Why not, Mom?" Davey said. "That's what we've both been wantin'."

What a blooper! We can't get a single station. I forgot to get an aerial. Seattle, the only station, is 150 miles away.

Christmas dinner at Vic and Myrt's. In the late afternoon, while the women chatted, I helped Vic remove a five-foot cedar stump from behind the house. A sweaty business. I am not sure whether it was the block and tackle, or his language, that loosened the roots.

VIC

Vic, a natural product of Salt Spring, has the toughness of a Garry oak with the internal sweetness of a wild strawberry. His five acres are an island on which he is Crusoe, bounded by three parts woods, one part sea. The sea is his lumberyard, dinner, and picture window; the timbers and shakes of his house and barn once grew on the hillside. Not a blade of grass or the smallest fir is unfamiliar to his intense blue eyes, which glow with depths of tenderness. He does his chores with a sort of careless enthusiasm, as if he loved them, with no undue concern for the weather, the weeds, or the hovering forest that ever threatens to reclaim the land. Like disciples, chickens and cats follow at his feet. He loves everything that lives, often feeding deer in the barn along with the cows. He is never in haste to plant the garden or sow alfalfa, yet he manages to market the first potatoes, and his hayloft is usually the earliest filled. Time is the only currency he has plenty of. It is not packaged into hours, but loosely bundled with love into children and neighbors, tides and seasons.

In the purest sense Vic is not a religious man, his holy trinity being "make over, make do, or do without." Though he is polite to "religion peddlars" who urge him to follow God's will, he claims that he needs no solace from views that are so much like his own. He loves the daily walk to deliver milk as well as to chat with neighbors. Salters look up to him as an oracle; to oblige, he assumes—thumbs tucked under his braces—the pontifical manner. One look at a pregnant sow brings a prophecy of the time and size of the litter, and a sharp squint at the June sky divulges when to bring in hay or to set out tomatoes. He knows nature's thoughts before she knows her own.

On more mundane matters—war, politics, and space travel—his thoughts have the flavor of fresh earth—eminently practical, as if he had plucked them from the soil like carrots and leeks. His life is built with homely virtues as much as with his hands. But it is not a simple life—rather a complex one, for it is filled with so much variety and richness.

THIS MORNING I reinforced the main float and stiffened the gangway; this afternoon, topped the giant fir behind the den and attached the TV antenna. After tea the four of us (Davey astride my shoulders) hiked to Panther Point. As we looked across to Salt Spring through the misty haze, Alice gasped, "You mean civilization is *that* far away!"

Jeanne smiled. "If you call it that."

In the evening, I read some of Arnold, some of Sainte-Beuve, with delight and no little awe, till past midnight, then dropped into bed feeling every part of me wonderfully spent. If there were only more days like these! How well Anaïs Nin put it: "I won't stop living to write."

A mother-in-law on the couch does change things. Normally our sex life is full of fun, but now every time the snoring stops—it is . . .

The kingfisher tells the world when the fishing is good. Like a grumpy blue-gowned judge, he sits on the piling ready to disperse his tidings to every tern and gull. How full of life he is—cocky as a jay and restless as a cougar, from his feathered topnotch to his quivery tail. No instrument is so sensitive as his perception. He is a prophet to every disturbance, a sentinel to every sight and sound. Oh, there he goes like a jet . . . SPLASH! With a shrill staccato cry, off he goes to the madrona to devour his prize.

ONE EVENING Alice said, "Dave, what you need is a birdbath. It would be easy. Why don't you make one?"

"What for?" I replied. "Water's everywhere."

"No bird wants to bathe in *salt* water," Alice reasoned. "They'd itch all over. After all, they picked your island to live on. Don't you think you owe them a decent bath?"

"Nonsense." I ignored her, deep in Sainte-Beuve. "There are eleven fresh water lakes on Salt Spring. It wouldn't take them five minutes to hop over for a bath."

But Alice persisted. "No self-respecting bird wants to fly to another island to bathe. The poor things—they might catch cold."

I shook my head absently and muttered, "Crows have been going back and forth to Salt Spring for years. I haven't seen one with a cold yet."

"Crows are different, Dave."

"They've got wings, haven't they?"

"That's not the point," Alice bristled, with pure logic. "Canaries, robins, and towhees are beautiful birds. Proud birds. They need a birdbath if they are to be happy, and sing."

If we had one of those saucepans on a pedestal, I argued, Kiki would have a banquet.

"Please, Dave." Jeanne touched my arm.

With that, I had to yield.

ON TUESDAY, the unveiling took place at the mortar box. I broke open the molds and set the saucer on what resembled a husky cigar stand. For functional concrete, it looked pretty good.

"Nice, eh?" I said to Alice. "Just what you ordered."

She stuck her finger skeptically into the saucer as if testing a cake.

"It won't do!"

I was stunned. "Why? It looks all right to me."

"Not deep enough," was her verdict. "The poor things will only get their feet wet."

How could anyone so naturally sweet be so damnably irritating!

"Alice, it just can't be done. You can't build a birdbath to fit *all* sizes of birds," I pleaded. "Let them splash water on themselves."

It was like trying to convince a stone wall. Her eyes glistened.

"You'll have to make another bath, Dave." She held out her hands. "About this deep. After all, we've got the pedestal. You might as well do it right."

I was ready to dump the whole works into the sea. Instead, for peace, I mixed another batch of concrete.

The next day, when the deeper saucer was finished, I consulted Alice.

"Perfect," she beamed. "Let's put it up."

We settled for a spot outside the kitchen window. "We'll be able to watch them from here," she said proudly.

At lunch came the first sign of trouble. Near the rose-bushes, Kiki crouched with a wild gleam in her eyes. Alice ran out whooping and hollering, scaring the poor robin more than fearless Kiki.

"You've got to do something with that miserable creature," she cried. "She'll kill every bird."

"It's her natural instinct," I pointed out. "You can't stop her from wanting a free meal."

"Oh, yes you can." Alice never lacked an answer. "We'll build a fence."

LAST NIGHT ON TV we invited Artur Rubinstein into our home. While he played Beethoven, Chopin, Schubert, and Liszt, we caught a glimpse of a warm, wonderful man. A man who has known tragedy and transcended it, a man of integrity, humility, and high spirits, whose spontaneity and style as a musician —as in life—seem to stem from a warm-blooded love of adventure.

"I want to risk," said Rubinstein, "to dare. I want to be surprised by what comes out. I want to enjoy it more than the audience. That way the music can bloom anew. It's like making love. The act is always the same, but each time it's different."

At the age of seventy-three he is still an unabashed romantic. "To be alive, to be able to speak, to see, to feel, to walk, to have houses, music, paintings—it's all a miracle. I have adopted the technique of living life from miracle to miracle."

For us, perhaps, the greatest miracle is Rubinstein.

FRIDAY. At last a beautiful, calm day. At Fernwood we waved good-bye to Alice as the taxi sped up the hill. With a touch of sadness, Jeanne said, "I think we'll miss her, don't you?"

I nodded. "Yes," I had to admit. "We've never had a nicer Christmas with so much fun."

WE ROWED the New Year in. It was a tipsy affair, for when we first started the custom the skiff was not as crowded. Now boy and dog, man and woman listen to the gentle dipping of the oars as the calendar runs out. Last night Kiki jumped aboard (much to Wallie's disapproval), and we pushed off into the silence of the night like an overloaded ark. The air was brittle with white frost, the fragrance of evergreens, and the small sounds of our secret journey. As the Chemainus Mill whistled, we stopped and listened. Overhead another celebration was going on. "Look!" I pointed. The aurora borealis rumbled and skyrocketed streaks of pale pink and purple across the starry sky.

NOTHING IS more precious to me than my mentors. I feel indeed fortunate that—when still very young, headstrong, and unruly—Allan Dartford found me in the nick of time, and after helping me over the threshold of puberty unharmed, went on to share with me his own exuberant joy and delight in all beauty and nobility. Over the years it has been my good fortune to continue to love and admire him as friend and counselor. As a humble Keats once penned:

> Ah! had I never seen
> Or known your kindness, what might I have been?
> What my enjoyments in my youthful years
> Bereft of all that now my life endears?

There were others—Dr. Frank Baxter, Floyd Ruch, and Lewis Allbee—to whom I am eternally grateful and whose memory freshens the spirit. However, in all honesty I must confess I cannot remember a thing they taught. For they themselves were the best lesson I ever learned.

Man is an emulating creature. If he is worthy, his worthiness will brush off on his children, his friends, and his community, and like a splash upon the water, the ripples will extend to all eternity. (That's the wonderful thing about teaching. One never knows where the ripples stop.)

IT HAS BEEN a mild January, and we are a little suspicious. When I went over after the milk and mail, Vic philosophized, "Winter is like a woman, son. If she ain't bother'n yuh none, she's jest thinkin' up ways to."

What revelations these islanders are! Each one a singular constellation beside which the world seems but a village. Like Renaissance man, Vic tills each day like a field. The crops he reaps are sufficiency and joy. Nature touches him—not in parks as it does the city dweller, but more as if he was a hub of a wheel—at all points of the day. She conspires with his temperament to give him character. His eccentricities are nature's own. A discarded stove, an aged car, rusting in the backyard grass are not unlike the mossy windfalls that litter the forest floor. No endeavor within need is beyond his grasp, no inner strength goes untapped. He is architect, builder, caretaker of his kingdom. Resourcefulness is his key; freedom its reward.

How various smells stir the emotions! Yesterday the violent westerly brought the Crofton pulp mill—the odor of rotten cabbages. It dislodged all my lofty thoughts. This morning the outboard fumes of the passing water taxi recalled the unpleasant stench and furor of freeways. After supper, the fumes of my well-being as I puffed a cigar ignited a tempest. "Can't you," Jeanne coughed, "smoke those stinky things outside?"

*

I am always amused at the haste and diligence with which I chase after facts to secure a truth. As if that were all it takes!

When I look up at the books on my shelves I am humbled by such high company. Tolstoy, Hazlitt, Rousseau—will I ever get to know them? If only I could control this yearning to educate myself. My mind is too curious, too greedy. It's frightening. I have traveled so deeply into Keats that I do not know how to extricate myself. I must learn to lie fallow. To slim the mind. "Discovery is nothing," warns Valéry. "The difficulty is to acquire what we discover."

A FREIGHTER is rumbling by, its machinery clanking and its lights twinkling through the firs like a city on the march. What continent will she touch next, I wonder; what seaport will end her journey? Hong Kong . . . Liverpool . . . Bremen? True, travel has its charm, but the homing instinct is strong in me. There is a keener perception than that of sight. Hawaii holds no fairer day or more picturesque beach than those a foggy morning conjures. Most people go abroad to escape the burden of themselves. I relish life too much to pay an agent to be relieved of it. A sleepless night affords me as much travel as a Cook's tour.

I need only to stretch my legs to enter the Parthenon, which, unlike the original, has fir columns instead of stone and a bit of a list as aged woodsheds do. Here I am Phidias; I split wood instead of marble, file an ax rather than a chisel —but the skill is relatively the same. The difference is that Greek art warms the spirit whereas mine warms the blood —and a house!

Ancient wonders cannot compare to the wonder of a man. Unlike the Pyramids or Roman aqueducts, his structure is more hidden than revealed, more beautiful within than without. For intimate knowledge of him, we must seek him on his own soil. Meet me at the pub or on the street corner, you face only a carbon copy. The original is laying flagstone on the island. My hearth is sacred, the genie by which I divine and expand my being. "No man is an island," said Donne. On the contrary, we are all islands in a common sea—each a map on which only the shores and rivers are marked, but whose interior for the most part is uncharted. These nine years on Wallace, I have made only token explorations. Why shouldn't I stay put and delve a little deeper?

A frightful gale all night. My mind seems swept clean of thought.

Only by continual effort can I write. I long for interruption, an excuse to drift—for Davey to burst through the door!

How much I miss making love in the woods! The mossy dell with ferns growing waist high, the scent of buttercups, the sun splashing our nakedness. It is not the same inside, between sheets. The outdoors doubles the wonder and beauty of the human body, the incredible sweetness and desire of the flesh. I am grateful and a little proud that my inaugural into this mystery was not in some scruffy motel, but on the bed of a desert floor amid scorching sun and hovering sagebrush. Nature itensifies and glorifies the sexual act. At the moment of climax we experience oneness with her as with our partner.

LAST DAY of January. What have I accomplished? Two chapters, a sore "peck" finger, the protest "Must you write *all* day?"

I wish that I could assemble notes of thought as beautiful as Chopin's Piano Concerto in E Minor—how I love it!

Today this quiet realization came to me: I am a man without a country. I should feel bitter and alienated, I suppose, but on the contrary, it's like a weight lifted from my shoulders. When someone says, "Oh, aren't you an American?" it jars me. I am instantly packaged, labeled, and politely dismissed.

The beauty of island life is that it bleaches out nearly all the impurities of what has gone before. It provides distance and quietude for value judgments. Thus, unknowingly, I have become an anachronism. I am a free man. Like a young gull who is no longer nestbound, but who has wings with which to soar and cares little what land he roams over or into which river, lake, or sea he swoops for fish. The island could as well be off the coast of Spain or Madagascar. For I am bounded by no system of things, no border except that of truth. America may have been the country of my birth, Canada the country where I live, but the country of my spirit is mankind.

Mankind, to me, is the individual. States, races, do not exist in my mind. I am patriotic only about what I love . . ."all that's high, and great, and good and healing." This vaster loyalty frees the human spirit of the obsolescent bonds of nationality and, like all true culture, makes us citizens of the world.

AN ARCTIC BLAST! Last night the thermometer dropped to twenty-two, and when I awoke this morning there came a shout from the kitchen, "Dave, there's no water."

I struggled into icy pants that could stand up by themselves, crawled under the house with the propane torch, and began to thaw the pipes. Disgruntled, I managed only to burn my gloves. Soon as I stepped in the door the smell of percolating coffee revived my spirits.

"We're lucky." Jeanne smiled rather triumphantly. "At least the well didn't freeze."

Snow is falling.
"Oh, boy!" Davey exclaimed.

Jeanne frowned. "Oh, no! We're in for it."
"Fun!" I cried. "Where's the sled, Davey?"

ON FEBRUARY 20: What a long cold spell. Two weeks now without running water, with blankets at the windows and the fireplace going full bore. Room temperature is a brisk forty-eight (no central heating!), and I write with long johns, wool shirt, and two sweaters on. The book—as yet untitled—is a real Matterhorn. I am a climber without rope, pick, or experience, feeling my way up the slopes. Two pages a day. The pitfalls are my syntax; participles dangle all over the page, and I never know when I climb over the bluff of a sentence which tense I'm in. For every step upward, it seems, I take two sideways—as each pretty view entices me to digress. But I'm learning—learning that writing is a dreadful encounter with the unknown. The depths of one's ignorance.

I heard the door open and Davey creep to my side. I kept typing, pretending that I hadn't noticed.
"Why do you use one finger, Papa?"
"Don't know. Suppose it's because I didn't have lessons."
"Must you have lessons?"
"No."
"How come you don't learn?"
That, I thought, was a good question.

In the evening I am reading *Midnight on the Desert,* which acts like a sedative and makes me wonder if Priestley doesn't spread himself too thin. So many first books are the best because the author writes from what he feels. From then on he drifts into what he only knows. It is a sad thing when talent improves and the affections decline. For every great classic is a rebound of love. "To write a novel," admitted Sainte-Beuve, "is merely my way of being in love and saying so." Like Sainte-Beuve and that "notorious leader of huckle-

berry parties," my books will be the record of my romances.
Yea, the pages but the days I give my heart away.

For me, the day is empty when I find nothing to embrace.
My heart is so greedy that I believe happiness lies not in contentment but in *ardor,* "a sort of magnificent using up," Gide
declares, "by which we are perpetually renewed." I tremble
on the verge of hedonism; everything excites my desire to
know—to enjoy. To seek the soul behind everything. This
insatiable curiosity will be my undoing! Not long ago I
foolishly risked crossing a turbulent channel hoping to discover a new biography of Keats in the mail.

THIS CRISP, SUNNY morning I was out early, shoveling paths,
while Davey and Wallie frolicked in the snowdrifts. They
rolled and wallowed, struggled to their feet, then rolled again.
Later Davey and I built a snowman: buttons for eyes, tri-
angular eraser nose, dark glasses—I even gave up my pipe.
Wallie reared on his haunches, suddenly barking and growling.
We choked with laughter.

What a delight to flesh out the bare bones of thought.
Winter's fruit! I long to collect some such specimens into a
book—an "almanac of mental moods." If it happens to please,
good. If not, it will serve as a fresh introduction to myself.

ALL DAY a drizzling rain. The drops are lashing the windows,
melting the snow into lakes, and swelling the streams into
brooks. "If this keeps up," I said at lunch, "I'll need a boat
to get to the den."

Humans are extremely adaptable creatures. A war more
than amply convinced me "you can get used to hell—if you
are there long enough." But one thing—even after years—
I haven't grown used to is rural mail delivery. (As Vic says
of a cow about to calf, "Ain't no way of tellin' when she'll

come.") It depends a lot on the acts of God—the time it takes to clear a tree from across the road; and a lot on the acts of a cranky Ford. More often than not, it depends on the acts of Mr. Norris, who is deeply moved by the question "Won't you come in for a nip of rye?"

IT'S DAVEY'S BIRTHDAY, and Jeanne is baking a cake. I can smell angelfood, his favorite! We have had quite a time hiding the pair of rabbits. Wallie discovered the box and knocked it over. We spent hours dislodging the woodpile to recover them.

At dinner a gala party—hats, favors, horns—and fur, when Kiki laid eyes on Imogene and Tanto! (Wallie was *not* invited.)

Dear David: Now that you are six, I am wondering tonight what I would say to you if you were sixteen. You see, I had no father, so I would speak to that young lad in myself as I would to you. Let me begin with this question: "What do a man, a mountain, and an ocean have in common?" One thing, David—infinite potential. The wonder of us all is our "could be."

But first, let us begin where God left off, after he gave us arms, legs, a brain. He gave us two things—will and inertia.

Man is a mixture. Mostly inertia, nonlife.

Will is the thrust of life.

Our task is to will ourselves into worthy beings. The human spore contains a thousand possibilities with which to build many I's. For man is like no other creature; he creates his "self." How does he accomplish this? By tapping those deep springs within himself so that they gush forth, pure and clear, rich with the minerals of goodness and joy. Life is infinite choice. The measure of our affections determines our unity, the richness of our souls. In choosing, we become.

As the lonely navigator plots his course by the stars, so,

DAVEY TRIES TO MAKE PEACE BETWEEN WALLIE AND TANTO

David, will your course be made luminous by your inner sky. We carry our destiny with us.

Each day is a dock from which we set sail to discover the realm of our future selves. The horizon holds no mystery, only a reality to be experienced. The fun of life is creating ourselves as we move along. It is not the destination that matters, but going toward.

The future is not for us to foresee, but to enable.

To build the future, think the present. The here and now.

Be not deceived, David, by the lure of happiness. It is a form of rest. A stopping. The absence of fever. Life bids us to rise and be set aglow. Men are known and famed by their *ardor,* the stretching that is natural to every soul. Without a longing, how does the seed push from the soil? How else do we go beyond ourselves—climb the distant hill?

David, you will soon start school. It is a place you go to learn how to educate yourself. Our learning commences after we leave the classroom. Mankind's past—from a moment ago—is your legacy. Consult the wealth of your heritage. It is a bank account that cannot be overdrawn.

However, it is not enough to read the pages of a history book. One must *feel* the words. Knowledge without feeling is like a car without gasoline. A fact, if it is to serve, must be felt upon the pulse and lie within the radius of some human need.

Science is a world of facts. In solving every mystery it has made man more of a mystery to himself. Thus, we know more of man from the poet than from the man of science. The poet's art, David, is the art of self-discovery. When a great poet speaks of himself, he speaks for mankind. I bid that reverence accompany you, for nothing enlarges us more than to be a pupil to the perfection of others. Every great soul owes its being to a worshipful nature.

But, David, shun no one's role. What each man aspires to is sufficient to itself. The radiance that shines from a finely knit quilt is no different from that which illuminates a canvas by Van Gogh. All that is good and beautiful originates from the same source: an act of love.

David, I will speak to you of love. For how else can you play those dormant melodies that reside in your heart? The worst poverty is not an empty belly, but an empty heart. Sickness of a wasted soul. Unused life. The anguish of not caring. For what is love but a lacking—an incompleteness by which we are fulfilled. Within every human breast lies a wealth of love. It not only creates opportunities but its own talents as well.

The most beautiful love is the love of life. More than anything, David, let me give you that love. In no other way can I bestow on you the joys that I have won. But to bestow love is to bestow hunger. Loving is a hungry heart. And so, David, I would have you hunger for daybreak. Sleep was made for night. The day was made for man. Worship its splendor. Taste it. Feel it. Do not the birds sing from its delight? Love and wonder are the conspirators of joy. Let the body and soul suffer from their conspiracy. Make every day a feast day—of the sweet and the splendid: the silvered spider's web; fog-shrouded firs, like pinnacles pointing toward God; the trillium's bloom; the autumn trail steeped in feathery gold.

The seasons, David, are like the calendar pages of the heart. The dry hot spells of our interior come and go like desert flowers, which raise their petals to the light. Their strength comes from heat as well as cold, from dryness as from the wet. Apples! Oh, the apples I have eaten swelled by the sun but owed their blush and tartness to the frost. Are not my summer thoughts pears which winter ripens? The harvest of guests reckoned on a winter's night? Every schoolboy knows it takes heat to produce cold. So, in a man, it takes cold to warm thought, heat to set the arctic regions of the heart aglow. As a taut bow springs the arrow, all vigor and creativeness spring from tension—the ebb and flow of opposites that stretch the soul.

David, consider the seed. The fir cone—how nature abandons itself to produce one tree! Abandon yourself likewise, my son. Let fervor multiply your seed. For all blossoming comes from fervor, love going its own wild way. It ignites every gleam, lights up every man. If our souls have been of any worth, said a wise man, it is because they have burnt more ardently than others.

THE FIRST DAFFODILS—and it was snowing a week ago!

What a strange paradox: with pick and shovel, you spend days breaking down a sea bank, more days hauling rock and gravel, and weeks building a wall to keep the sea from stealing chunks of the island. Overnight, frost cracks the joints and, the following day, a gale brings up battering rams. Wham! Huge drift logs seek to smash the wall to bits. When the wind subsides and the sun pops out, as you're patching the damage a short, stumpy man with a briefcase appears. A gleam rushes into his eyes. Zoom! Up go your taxes!

The assessment notices came in today's mail. We stared at the figures—twice what it cost to build. I groaned. "Something is wrong with a system that penalizes hard work, improving your property, and getting the most from a bag of cement!"

THERE'S A SUCCESSION of days now that have the quality of fine crystal, so exquisite they make up for the whole year's atmospheric delinquencies.

Beachcombing this afternoon, picking men's minds tonight. What a royal feast the world is to the inquisitive mind! Whether it's on the shores of the island or the shores of literature, beachcombing is the most delightful occupation I know. I am a scavenger at heart like our crows—an apple one moment, a starfish the next. My tidbits have been Toynbee and Emerson; the former divulges the currents that ebb and flow in mankind; the latter, the currents that ebb and flow in a man. They give full account of my own natural history.

Books and sea, library and shoreline have the same effect on me. They satisfy my urge to plunder, a sort of privileged lawlessness that enables me to loot the wealth of the human race. By day and by night, I am a pirate—greedy and unmerciful.

The mind bulges with knowledge, as the storage shed bulges with booty. In both places, the trophies lie stacked by the hundreds, nearly forgotten and without any apparent use. Racks hold doors, butter boxes, nets, sea-dressed planks of miscellaneous sizes and shapes that may be oak, fir, mahogany, or cedar. My notebooks overflow with thoughts, ideas, truths, bits of wisdom—on a variety of subjects, majestic and minute. Such wealth arouses the latent creator. Last winter a fourteen-foot gaff-rigged sailer was built in the lounge and returned to the sea from whence it sprang. Another winter will give birth to a book that will owe its generating force and inspiration to the beach of literature. Everything the sea gives forth is eventually useful. An old broom handle is a clothes rack; kelp fertilizes the garden. Likewise, the great legacy of knowledge that washes ashore in books.

IT'S NEARLY MARCH, and already there are pussy willows on the way to the wharf.

We have moved from the bedroom onto the porch. The double bed fits between the kitchen and porch windows so snugly that we must climb in over the foot.

"Now that Davey's school age," Jeanne remarked, "he should have his own room." That meant our room—the only bedroom.

THE VIEW FROM OUR BED ON THE PORCH

We have long pondered his schooling. Neither of us believes that parents make good teachers, or that school by correspondence is the answer. Most of all, Davey needs playmates.

"Did you know," Jeanne said one evening, "he has two imaginary friends? Felix and Browse. I wormed it out of him when I saw him talking to himself on the wharf. The poor tike is lonely. He'll love school, I'm sure."

"Still think I can run him over every day," I said. Vic brought the school bus right to Fernwood.

Jeanne did not look up. "You know the channel." She paused. "We'll see."

*

A record—five weeks now since I've seen a soul. Jeanne and Davey have been going over after the milk and mail. My work forges ahead in speed and delight with the spells of quite empty days before me. The outer life, it seems, must lie fallow if the creative one is to flower.

You write with your *whole* being. No fears. No falseness. Those will be your best words.

Six hours at the saga.
An hour at the woodpile.
An hour of wilderness.
An hour with R. Crusoe and Davey.
A moonlight ramble to Sunrise Cove.
A few pages of Ruskin; the fierce ecstasy of love.
So goes the day.

A CORMORANT on the rocks sits like a black-gowned nun with arms outstretched. What a miscarriage of justice evolution has perpetrated. We are told birds sprang from reptiles. The cormorant has not quite made the leap. Somewhere in the glacial mists of the past, part of his genetic makeup passed into hypnotic slumber. He has the webbed feet of water birds but not their moistureproof feathers, and though a fish diver, he will drown if he does not go ashore regularly to dry them.

The cormorant is the dunce of all bird creation. He is incapable of uttering an intelligent birdlike sound, and barren of the most basic urge—the will to fight. Crows steal his eggs while he sits dumbly on the nest. Gulls force him from the choicest nesting grounds. Eagles fly off unchallenged with his young. And if he were more tasty—they would add him to their diet. Had it not been for man's protection, he'd long since have gone the way of the dinosaur.

Like an outcast, the cormorant dwells on dry reefs and scraggly islets. From a distance, the colonies appear like black

CORMORANTS ON A MISTY WINTER MORNING

upthrusts of sea bottom. I go to these forlorn shreds of land to gather guano. If you can stand the stench, flies, and mites, there is no finer fertilizer. A sagacious gardener, Dr. Mac rows several miles for a pailful. Each time I am saddened by their permissiveness and their haphazard nests—bits of flotsam and seaweed—that cling precariously to the rocks, and I come away marveling at their survival.

I have a special fondness for the cormorant—not because my begonias have the fairest blooms, but because he is an underdog. Commonly referred to as shags—a deprecatory title man has assigned to him—he has succeeded only in one sphere. He is an expert fisherman, the envy of every seabird, which is the reason the Japanese use him as a fishline. In fact, he is such an eager fisherman that he often forgets his plimsoll line.

As I watch him closely, I see the sadness in his profile —his silence and unbirdlike stance. A lonely sentinel in funeral black, he sits like some unknowing stranger from another world. The tragic beauty of his repose lingers hauntingly in the mind. I can see man reflected in this awkward yet noble bird. We, like him, are both beautiful and terrible failures. We have not won our true nature; the cormorant has not won his. We are not animal, not fully man. If I am to believe Chardin, our biological evolution has run its course, but our spiritual has only begun.

Ever since man left the leafy curtain of the jungle and appeared upright on the plains, his struggle for human status has been a precarious thing. Brute and human still wage battle in the depths of our subconscious. Like a water glider, we are suspended on fragile film between freedom and catastrophe. Have we come too far too fast? Become mindless robots in a technological junkyard?

We have, in truth, a rope of cleverness around our necks. Knowledge, science, reason have neither freed nor humanized us. "There must be," said Thoreau, "the copulating and generating force of love behind every effort destined to be successful." As love serves to complete and fulfill one man, so it will complete and fulfill mankind. Therein lies our hope, if only we grasp it.

RAIN OR SHINE, the best hour of the day is when I plunge into the woods. This afternoon the wilderness bore unexpected fruit—a beautiful title: *Once Upon an Island*. Will I be able to make the chapters as beautiful?

On second thought, as Winfield Townley Scott once said:

BABY SEA GULLS

"Not to make something 'beautiful' but something *true*—which in time will be beautiful."

SPRING IS PROBING the island. There is much duck talk, wing-flapping, and cavorting going on in the cove. A sudden intoxication grips the air. Gulls are pairing off. The bush is alive with twittering. Mink have grown more gregarious, more tolerant, and more noisy. A lonely raven's urgent cry drifts among the firs. Along the seabanks maples are pushing into foliage, wild currant is a blaze of red, and carpets of bluebells hug the sparse pockets of soil. Under the trees salal is greening, bracken unfurling. Fir limbs are aglow with chartreuse tips. Everywhere throbs the pulse of growth. Silent, strong, ceaseless. Am I—I wonder—growing too?

What pleasure and pain I feel glancing through my journal. All together, the pages disturb me. Not so much what I say but *how* I say it. Must I always be a moralist? Can't I put across a point or convey an anecdote without preaching? How simple it is to be self-righteous when self-employed; virtuous, when you are solitary. You can be bold and legislate for mankind, for you have never felt the tyranny of the timeclock, the torment of a demanding boss, or wondered seriously where the next meal would come from. You love life because it has not bruised you. You feel honored and exceptional, good and strong in your castle. Vain little man!

THIS MORNING Davey and Wallie are fishing in front of the house. They have orders not to stand up in the rowboat, which Davey understands. Not Wallie. Every time the pole nods, he's on all fours, the boat careening as he peers overside. He is completely oblivious to the hazards of boating as well as the sound of the human voice. Because Jeanne has grown hoarse, we have had to adopt sterner measures, and I have had to adopt earplugs. Now, when Wallie's snout rises above the gunnel, Jeanne blows the police whistle and Wallie collapses into a mass of quivering flesh.

WHAT COURAGE and integrity one finds in Keats! If only my admiration would give me the discipline to pull myself up to

WALLIE AND DAVEY GO FISHING IN FRONT OF THE HOUSE

the level of my reverence. It is so true, as Ruskin says, that reverence is the chief joy and power of life—"reverence for that which is pure and bright in our youth, for what is true and tried in the age of others; for all that is gracious among the living, great among the dead, and marvelous in the Powers that cannot die."

THE CENSUS QUESTIONNAIRE that came today has me in a quandary. I did fine until I reached the little block that asked: "What is your occupation?" Try as I may, I haven't yet been able to answer it—honestly, that is. Since the resort is merely

OILING THE GENERATOR

IN THE STORE

CHECKING THE FRESH-WATER TANK

SETTING OUT FROM THE WORKSHOP

a facade that conceals a dozen or so pursuits—which might be defined in union circles as illegal practices—I am wishing for once I was a clean-cut man, a simple milkman, salesman, or businessman.

Actually, I am just a landlord who rents summer cottages, and I suppose our little grocery makes me a storekeeper of sorts. Because I grow and sell fruit and vegetables, I could be considered a farmer—a table farmer, at least. Since I built the house, cottages, and wharf (so I like to believe), after a fashion I am a carpenter. The guests who try to make the built-in beds or to open the sliding windows may think otherwise. Though I installed the pipes, sinks, showers, and toilets, I am more often than not reminded that I should not have. People need only one scalding to realize I plainly am no plumber—that the hot and cold taps are reversed. As a mechanic, I fare better. I manage to keep the boats, machinery, and pumps going. But I haven't as yet cured the epidemic of power failures that always occurs in summer. A generating plant is a little peculiar—a little like me, I suppose. It runs best when there are no people around.

But I think it is as a nurseryman that I receive the greatest pleasure and take the greatest pride. What nursery has a stock of three million firs, one million hemlock, half a million cedars and madronas, not counting thousands of oak, balsam, yew, willows, and maples? At the wharf the nursery shop is open night and day (in the fullest sense). It consists of six tiers of driftwood planks with an assortment of potted young trees and shrubs. They are self-watering from the overhead sprinkling system, and each plant is priced for self-service. A money box is nailed to a specimen tree nearby. At times I feel guilty that I have so large a spread and employ only one gardener, and that he keeps so busy we never see him.

The occupation that is the most bother and brings in the least money is that of marina operator—a fancy title

Americans have coined for the simple and more honest word, wharfinger. The sign on the float reads:

MOORAGE

Up to 20 feet—$1.50
20 to 30 feet—$2.00
Over 30 feet—$3.00
Please pay at the house

People won't cheat you on a five-dollar yew, but they will resort to any subterfuge to avoid paying two bucks to tie up overnight.

Force of circumstance, I admit, has made me a boat-builder rather than a boat-buyer. When Vic's beetle brows spotted our snappy red and white rental boats, he exclaimed, "Holy tin pots! Where did ja git the navy?" This makes me an admiral of no little distinction—of three motorboats, two rowboats, a sailboat, a kayak, and a leaky canoe.

I am also a fishing guide, for guests pay me to catch them salmon, which I confess is a lot more profitable to me than to them. However, my status as a professional photographer has slipped considerably, since both habit and Graflex suffer from disuse. Yet my first trade, that of laborer, has stood me well. I have been a seagoing Sherpa ever since I fled the Hod Carriers Union, Local 252, ten years ago. As a librarian I am self-employed, but professionally retired—except during summer when the resort library (my own books) begins to diminish; then I become a nasty shepherd on the prowl for lost sheep. Lastly, I put words on paper, which, in some literate circles, makes me a writer—I think.

I turned to Jeanne. "What am I?"

She thought for a moment. "Husband, father, and provider." Then she smiled. "And lover."

On the form, I wrote simply: Handyman.

THE YEAR has come full circle. As I look back, it is with a deep sense of gratitude and a feeling of selfishness for hoarding so large a measure of peace, freedom, and beauty. Yet, to me, they are the real trinity: peace—to know the self; freedom —to find the self; and beauty—with which to make the self. Wherever you find these the good life abounds, whether a river flows in front of your door, or the tide.

Island living bestows many privileges, but for none am I more grateful than the continual awareness that I am alive. When I gaze at the cove that draws the sea into the land, then exhales it like a deep breath, I do not feel the rhythm of nature's pulsebeat so much as my own. As I write, March is the chill that grips my legs, the unseen hand that rattles the windows and whips the channel feathery white. It is something felt, heard, and seen—not merely a leaf on the calendar pad of time.

As a student and celebrant of life, I grow quickly drunk on sunshine, a whiff of sea, the soft, tender flesh of a woman's body. The only real stimulant my aliveness needs is challenge. A stretching of soul. For aliveness is growth. It is openness to experience, like that of the young gull discovering his wings. It is courage to be what you are—as bold as what you dream. It is the joy that rises like the sun as morning awakes you. These are the things the island teaches—what I call the gifts of love. And loving and living go hand in hand.

However, as Jeanne says, "Nothing comes easy on an island." An outdoor life is not a "simple life" if you dislike work. What you earn seldom covers your labor or pays the grocery bill. Your remuneration is based on a nobler currency —the capacity to enjoy. I am not of this world, but another, when I step outdoors. The deer that sips from the forest pond is not the only one who thirsts. Nor does the bald eagle, in its aerial play, perform alone. My mind climbs upward, traveling from its roots like a branching fir in the silent, roofless, air. As Byron declares:

> I live not in myself, but I become
> Portion of that around me.

I am no "nature nut"—merely a second-class Crusoe who humbly believes that man, like a tree, is happiest outdoors. He is the natural partner to the earth, the sea, and the sky; when he loses contact with them, he loses an essential part of himself. Personally, I find abiding satisfaction and warmth in knowing that I am part of something older, wiser, and more permanent than man himself; that the periphery of my life has a definite order and wholeness, which cannot be changed or mutilated by any human being. There is both security and joy in the awareness that my hands are the finest tools; and that here, amid God's plenty, I can pasture my soul freely without the distraction of progress.

Editor's Note

The author's *Once Upon an Island* was published in 1967 and has since been translated into six languages. The Conovers have sold the resort, which is no longer in operation, and built a home on Princess Harbor. Their son, David, now grown up and married, is a male nurse. The author is working on more island adventures: *Sitting on a Salt Spring*.